THE COURAGE
TO BECOME

THE COURAGE TO BECOME

The Virtues of Humanism

Paul Kurtz

PRAEGER

Westport, Connecticut
London

Library of Congress Cataloging-in-Publication Data

Kurtz, Paul, 1925–
    The courage to become : the virtues of humanism / Paul Kurtz.
      p.   cm.
    Includes bibliographical references and index.
    ISBN 0–275–95897–3 (alk. paper). — ISBN 0–275–96016–1 (pbk.)
    1. Humanistic ethics. I. Title.
    BJ1360.K785   1997
    171′.2—dc21   96–53940

British Library Cataloguing in Publication Data is available.

Library of Congress Catalog Card Number: 96–53940
ISBN: 0–275–95897–3
     0–275–96016–1 (pbk.)

First published in 1997

Praeger Publishers, 88 Post Road West, Westport, CT 06881
An imprint of Greenwood Publishing Group, Inc.

Printed in the United States of America

The paper used in this book complies with the
Permanent Paper Standard issued by the National
Information Standards Organization (Z39.48–1984).

10 9 8 7 6 5 4 3 2 1

Intelligence is necessary to overcome foolishness. But it is not sufficient to tame fanaticism. Only courage can do that. A handful of men who are prepared to fight, to bleed, to suffer and, if need be, to die, will always triumph.

> Sidney Hook, *In Defense of Academic Freedom*
> (New York: Pegasus, 1971)

To save the world requires faith and courage—faith in reason, and courage to proclaim what reason shows to be true.

> Bertrand Russell, *The Autobiography*
> (Boston: Little, Brown and Company, 1967)

Scientific knowledge, and the human rationality that produces it, are, I believe, always fallible, or subject to error. But they are, I believe, also the pride of mankind. . . . Scientific knowledge is, despite its fallibility, one of the greatest achievements of human rationality.

> Karl R. Popper, *The Myth of the Framework*
> (New York: Routledge, 1994)

Contents

Acknowledgments

I wish to thank Timothy J. Madigan, Thomas Flynn, and Matthew Cherry for reading portions of this manuscript and providing constructive criticism. All three are heroic champions of the secular humanist outlook. I am especially grateful to Ranjit Sandhu for his invaluable help in preparing this manuscript for publication.

Prologue

This book is an essay on humanism. It is an attempt to explicate the basic moral virtues of humanism.

Humanists cherish a pluralistic set of virtues or excellences. These virtues are related to the "common moral decencies." By these I mean the basic principles that a morally developed person will recognize as worthy in human society. They are the key ethical principles that ought to be respected by everyone. The common moral decencies are hard won. They have evolved over a long period of human history. They cut across cultural differences and provide common grounds of shared human interests and needs. Although recognized as morally binding by civilized societies, they need to be constantly reinforced by both reason and emotion, to be cultivated in the young by moral education, and to become part of the character traits of mature persons—as Aristotle recognized. Most (if not all) of the common moral decencies are accepted by humanists and theists alike. They need not derive their authority from theological or metaphysical foundations; they are tested in human experience and reaffirmed by their consequences in behavior.

The common moral decencies apply primarily to our relationships with other human beings living in communities. I list them here, but without any further elaboration: (1) integrity—truthfulness, promise-keeping, sincerity, honesty; (2) trustworthiness—fidelity, dependability; (3) benevolence—good will, nonmalfeasance as applied to persons, nonmalfeasance as applied to private and public property, sexual consent, beneficence; (4) fairness—gratitude, accountability, justice, tolerance, cooperation.[1]

There are still other virtues or excellences that humanists advocate and that apply primarily to individuals in their own personal lives. When properly developed, these moral virtues enable individuals to pursue lives of creative and joyful exuberance. I again list these virtues here but without further explication: autonomy, intelligence, self-discipline, self-respect, creativity, motivation, affirmation, health, *joie de vivre*, and aesthetic appreciation. They are the virtues of free and independent individuals who make their own choices and guide their own destinies. The entire set of moral virtues, if implemented, can contribute to individual happiness, social harmony, and the public good.

I have elsewhere described humanism as a *eupraxophy* (good wisdom and practice).[2] By this I mean that humanism expresses a distinctive nonreligious life-stance. Specifically, it advocates a cosmic outlook based upon science and philosophy and a practical ethical approach to the good life. Unlike theoretical science, which seeks to explain how nature operates, or pure philosophy, which is concerned with analysis, eupraxophy attempts to apply knowledge to practical normative issues. I especially wish to contrast humanistic eupraxophy with both transcendental theistic religion, which often considers the highest moral virtues to be faith, hope, and charity, and the skeptical nihilistic attitude, which denies that there are any objective grounds for the moral virtues.

---

1 . For a fuller elaboration see Paul Kurtz, *Forbidden Fruit: The Ethics of Humanism* (Amherst, N.Y.: Prometheus Books, 1988).

2 . See Paul Kurtz, *Eupraxophy: Living without Religion* (Amherst, N.Y.: Prometheus Books, 1989).

Prologue

Humanistic eupraxophy denies the existence of a theistic universe, and it likewise rejects the hopelessness and despair of nihilism. As such, it emphasizes three pivotal moral virtues or excellences: *courage*—to persevere and overcome; *cognition*—critical thinking and ethical rationality; and *caring*—compassion and benevolence. These are related to the entire constellation of virtues and are perhaps even foundational to them.

In the course of writing this book I have come to realize that of these three moral excellences, courage, in some way, is the most important, and that is why I have entitled this book *The Courage to Become*. In one sense, it is written in response to the postmodernist critique of reason and science, its widespread rejection of humanistic values (such as freedom and autonomy) and its loss of confidence in the ability of humankind to solve its problems. I submit that the courage to create our futures is the defining characteristic of the entire human enterprise, both individually and socially. This is central to the humanist outlook—although courage is closely related to the human capacity to reason, and it is infused by a compassionate and benevolent humanistic concern for the needs of others. How and why I think that courage, cognition, and caring are so vital will be developed in the course of the following argument, into which I invite the reader to enter.

Chapter 1

The Human Prospect

THE QUEST FOR MEANING

The question is sometimes raised, What is the human prospect? In other words, What place does human life, my life or your life, or that of our society have in the grand scheme of things? People who ponder this question often ruminate about the human condition, the nature of tragedy, or human existence as viewed from the eye of eternity. They wonder whether the aspirations and achievements of humans can find safe haven in the universe at large. They yearn for immortality for themselves and their loved ones.

Alas, the testimony from everyday life and the evidence of the sciences hardly supports the vain hope that human life has any special ontological anchor in reality, or that humans will exist in some idyllic future state of immortality. Life can be wonderful, but the brutal fact is that each individual at some time must die. Indeed, the human species is only one among many life forms that have emerged on planet Earth. We are not necessarily the highest form of life, nor can we discern any progressive path to the evolutionary process. How long the human species will survive in the future is uncertain; yet we are prone to create gods in our own image and to think the universe is made for us, or that we, unlike other species, have a special place reserved for us in eternity.

The Copernican and Darwinian revolutions are a blow to human pride; we have been dethroned from the conviction that we are the center of a universe that was created for us and the belief that we are fundamentally different from all other species. Many still refuse to accept the full implications of these discoveries. The evidence from astronomy points to the fact that someday all life on our planet will become extinct. The earth when viewed from outer space appears to be a resplendent blue-green dot. That our planet will continue as it has, encircling our sun forever, hospitable to variegated life forms, is doubtful. It is hurtling through space at an incredible speed. One can imagine and even predict the eventual running down of our solar system. Our sun, on the edge of the Milky Way, is one of an estimated billion trillion suns—more than all of the sands on all of the beaches of the world. The universe is a vast spectacle of galaxies, explosively hot at first, then cooling off and dying. The evidence presently points to a cosmic explosion in the distant past—the Big Bang. How and why that occurred and what preceded it is unknown. Moreover, in time our sun will probably cool down and all life forms on Earth will perish. There are other solar and planetary systems throughout the galaxies, some perhaps like ours, supporting a rich panoply of life forms. We exist in a universe virtually infinite in space and unfathomable in time; it is more extensive than we can comprehend. To claim that it exists *for us* or that God has created us in his own image is presumptuous *chutzpah* in its most inflated form.

To pose the abstract question in general: What is *the* human prospect? is grandiloquent; it makes little sense unless one phrases it in concrete spatial-temporal terms. We should ask, *from what vantage point*—my frame of reference here and now; or the recorded memory of our society, perhaps two or five or ten centuries in scope; or from a broader archaeological scale, say one hundred or five hundred centuries? And how far do we peer into the future—one century or fifty? It is hard enough knowing what will happen twenty years from now, let alone a thousand. Accordingly, it is difficult to respond to the question of the human prospect in purely theoretical terms. For each prospect in history is unique, and the varieties of human life that have or will exist always are at critical turning points. A person *can* ask, What is the prospect for me or my country, or perhaps even world civilization at any one time in history?

I can imagine the question asked retrospectively: What was the prospect of my great-grandfather when he immigrated to America from Saint Petersburg, Russia, in 1880? Or what was the prospect of *his* great-grandfather who was a grenadier in Napoléon's grand army as it invaded Russia? The French army was defeated, and my forebear was left stranded in Russia, where his offspring remained for seventy years before leaving for America. What about *his* great-grandfather, who presumably lived in early eighteenth-century France? And so we can go backwards in time. We can pose the questions imaginatively for anyone at any time in the past: What were the prospects of victory for Socrates as he stood trial in Athens; or of Xerxes as he assembled his army to invade Attica; or of Eisenhower and the Allied forces as they were ready to cross the English Channel in the Second World War; or of the population of Hiroshima in 1945 as the Enola Gay prepared to drop the first atomic bomb?

More specifically we can ask of anyone, What were *your* prospects at the age of eighteen, and how many of them will be fulfilled at seventy; and what are your prospects, financially and medically, now? What were the prospects of your country at various points in history as it faced the challenges of recession, civil strife, and war? What will be the prospects of your children and their children's children's children? We can ask retrospectively a large-scale question, How did our forebears adapt to the onslaught of the Ice Age with the climactic changes that this caused in human behavior? And prospectively, How will human civilization face possible global warming, pollution, or other catastrophes as yet unseen?

There are always contingent, contextual problems faced by human beings and human civilizations. When we are reflecting on human prospects, these should be interpreted pluralistically, concretely, and contextually. The spectacle of human history reveals a virtually infinite variety of prospects. The drama of human life is unpredictable, as human dreams and expectations are realized or shattered. At any one moment, the future is either promising or foreboding. The vista beyond is unclear; we may be inspired or frightened by what lies around the next corner or far down the road. We constantly wonder about what awaits us: victory or defeat, prosperity or adversity, achievement or failure. It all depends on the specific context of one's *lebenswelt* (life world).

HUMANISM VERSUS ANTI-HUMANISM

No doubt those who are in a quandary about the human prospect are thinking in cosmic terms, and they are looking for some guarantee that we all will be rescued from our finitude. Does the universe have a purpose? Is there any deeper meaning for human life? If there is no discernible purpose to human existence, and if nature is ultimately indifferent to our fondest hopes and deepest aspirations, what is left for us? If we are all dead in the end, why does anything matter?

These are the perennial questions one ponders when confronted with the fragility of the human condition and one's own mortality. Experiencing failure, illness, conflict, the death of friends or family, or other tragedies only intensifies a person's longings for answers to these root questions. Every human being has to cope with the challenges of life. As we encounter the vicissitudes of fortune and realize the constant struggle necessary to realize our ends, we seek to piece these strands together into a meaningful framework. Do they have any deeper meaning? Or is it all "a tale told by an idiot, full of sound and fury, signifying nothing"?[1]

---

1 . William Shakespeare, *Macbeth*. In *The Works of Shakespeare* (New York: The Macmillan Company, 1905), vol. 3.

8

I wish to discuss three major responses to the quest for meaning: humanism, transcendental theism, and skeptical nihilism.

The first, known as *humanism*, is, I submit, virtually synonymous with what it means to be *human*: pluck and audacity, the will to survive and thrive. The humanistic outlook has pervasive roots in human history. It focuses on the need for self-reliant striving. Humanism seeks to portray the human condition in realistic terms, though very few individuals are able to face the brute character of existence: the fact that the universe at large is blind to our deepest expectations and darkest fears, that there is no teleological purpose discoverable in the nature of things, and that there is no conscious exaltation or grieving by nature *per se* if any particular organism or species fails or succeeds in its ventures, survives or dies. The scientific evidence points to the fact that the human species, like other forms of life on this planet, is a product of evolutionary processes. It has persisted as a result of adaptation; however, it has also benefited from Lady Luck. Survival is due to mutations, adaptations, and selective reproduction, which enables individuals to transmit their genes to their offspring and thus influence the course of evolution. Life is multifarious, assuming many forms; which of these diverse species will win out is a result of genetic roulette, order and chance, causal regularities and fortune. Whether humankind itself survives in the long run is doubtful. Like the saber-toothed tiger, the dinosaur, or the many extinct exotic species embedded in the Canadian Burgess shale, the human species may one day be decimated by blight or destruction, a plague or meteor collision, or some other untoward disaster. What will happen depends in part on what we do. Our efforts are inextricably tied to our ability to cope with challenges in the natural and social environment. In the long run there is no surcease from our labors undertaken to survive, and no ultimate guarantee that we will.

The "patron saint" of humanism is the ancient mythological character Prometheus, who challenged the gods on high, stole fire, and bequeathed to humankind the arts and sciences of civilization—so that we need not huddle in fear and tremble in caves, as did primitive men and women, but that we might go forth, taking destiny into our own hands, and overcoming the limits of our animal natures. This form of exultant humanism is an expression of optimism. Although aware of our fragile finitude, the brute fact of our mortality recedes into the background of our consciousness. Humans resolve to leave their imprints on nature, to bend it where possible to suit their desires. The plans and projects that we conceive of and strive to bring into being are expressions of the dreams and ideals that inspire us.

Humanists do not grieve for the "human condition"; neither do they have an exaggerated sense of the tragic, nor are they wont to demean human worth. They advise us to be *courageous*, to use our best talents, especially our rational powers, to understand the natural causes of things, and to focus on ways of resolving problems. They are not weighed down by the belief that this life is a vale of tears, nor do they moan for salvation. They are determined to persevere and to overcome adversities. Optimistic humanists exude a positive outlook; they may even at times be exuberant. In any case humanists affirm the possibility of the good life here and now; they believe that human suffering can be ameliorated and the problems of life overcome by human efforts. They advise both individual enterprise and cooperative action in order to mitigate evils and attain social justice. Promethean humanists emphasize that each of us has only one life to live, that we should not waste it but live it fully, sharing our joys with others. Prometheans depend on human powers; they cherish initiative and independence, discovery and invention; they herald human freedom and personal autonomy. They focus on the achievement motive, and they applaud creative energy, mighty works, and splendid deeds. They recognize that among the highest pleasures and joys of life are those shared with others; these are intrinsic to the good life and can be savored and enjoyed for their own sake. A person eventually learns that his or her own personal fulfillment is tied up with the fulfillment of others, and he or she comes to recognize the need to work cooperatively with others in order to build a more harmonious society. As a social animal, he or she eventually appreciates the obligation to be reasonable and morally responsible, empathetic and caring, and to cultivate the arts of negotiation and cooperation. Although every individual is on one's own—it is *his* or *her* life to create or destroy—we are what we are as part of a community of persons, and our highest ideals are realized within the parameters of society and culture.

The Promethean attitude came to fruition in the pagan world of Greco-Roman culture; it reappeared in the Renaissance when humanistic values were liberated from repressive medieval spirituality; and it has been going strong in the modern era where science and technology are used to improve the human condition. The Enlightenment project still needs to be fulfilled: to create a better world based on reason and the ideals of freedom and progress. The modern humanist is a *secular* humanist who does not believe in God or God's saving grace, but rather believes in human potentiality for achieving the good life. The goal is maximizing the conditions for the creative fulfillment of each individual and the achievement of joyful exuberance and happiness here and now.

There is a second fundamentally different response to the quest for meaning: the *theistic response*. This begins by denying our apparent finitude and defeat by death. It holds forth the prospect that there is a hidden purpose to reality and an ultimate meaning to human existence. This response involves a leap of faith, goaded on by what I have called the "transcendental temptation,"[2] that is, the human tendency to believe in a transcendent world beyond, and to seek a solution to human finitude by postulating a transcendental reality that will save us from the finality of death.

In one way or another this approach to the human condition is anti-humanistic. Extremely pessimistic about human power, it is grounded in denial; it seeks to persuade us that we do not have the power to control our destiny, that we are weak and depend-

---

2 . Paul Kurtz, *The Transcendental Temptation: A Critique of Religion and the Paranormal* (Amherst, N.Y.: Prometheus Books, 1986).

ent creatures, and that we can only be rescued in the end by a divine being or higher power. This attitude denies that the universe is impersonal, and it is based on a belief that there is a spiritual key to our destiny. Theists invent tales and parables, promising eternal life. The transcendent reality, they allege, exists beyond the world of reason and the senses. Theists yearn to be released from the trials, tribulations, and tragedies of life. They do so by convincing themselves that God has created the universe and will save us from oblivion. Death, they affirm, is not real; for we can live again in the future and attain eternal bliss.

Religious believers who depend upon "revelation" as the ultimate source of inspiration clothe the divine in human attributes. They believe that God appeared in history to various prophets, setting forth a path for righteousness and salvation. The puzzling characteristic of this theistic approach is that in fashioning God in human terms—for example, as Jesus, a human person, capable of suffering, atonement, and redemption by his Father—religion really has created a *human*, not a divine, solution to the existential dilemma of life. It offers a poetic, moral message that is out of cognitive touch with the real world; it is woven out of fantasies that embody the hopes and fears of human beings.

There are surely variations on this classical transcendental response. Some theists are so overcome by their duties to God, and their expectations of reunion with the divine presence, that they are willing to withdraw from this world in monastic solitude, constant prayer, or mortification. They will "render unto Caesar the things which are Caesar's" as they retreat into mysterious reverence and spiritualistic excursions. Some transcendentalists—Buddhists and Hindus, for example—focus on mystic release and tend to emphasize the passive state of acquiescence, freedom from desire and striving. Still others have one eye on the next life, but their feet planted in worldly affairs. Although concerned about the transcendental realm, they believe that they need to go about the business of living. These religionists build churches and temples to fulfill God's word, but they also apply their enterprise to help fashion a better secular world. For example, the Puritan virtues of thrift and hard work ensure that one's duties to the world are never forgotten.

The transcendental response assumes different expressions—from the religion of Isis and Osiris, to that of Krishna, Buddha, Moses, Jesus, or Mohammed, and various forms of modern-day spirituality. Nonetheless, these hold that man is finite, that our ultimate duty is submission to the divine will, that we can be saved only by devoting our lives to the higher spiritual power. In any case they are pessimistic about the ability of human beings by themselves to achieve a full creative life here and now, but they have a naïve cosmic optimism that humankind's destiny ultimately will be realized in a final, spiritual realization.

There is still a third response to the question of the meaning of life, and that is the posture of the *skeptical nihilist*. Skeptical nihilists agree with humanists that there is no evidence that God exists, or that there is a separable immortal soul, or a divine scheme of salvation. But they also infer that there is no humanist foundation for human ethics or social justice either. All values in the last analysis are subjective, a question of caprice and taste. Nihilists are often depressed by what they encounter in life. They are disillusioned by the bitter pill of existential reality that they are forced to swallow but cannot digest. All of our projects will fail inevitably, they say, for in the end we all must die. This may lead a person to despair, and perhaps even suicide. There is no real hope for humankind, nihilists declare. The reality principle, they believe, can inhibit motivation. It undermines the enthusiasm for living and the gusto for achievement. Nihilists insist that all knowledge is subjective and all values are relative. Because there are no Truths, it is passion and the will-to-power that eventually prevail in the human domain. This approach is anti-humanistic, for the nihilists not only do not believe in God but also have little or no faith in the abilities of us humans to solve our problems or the possibility for genuine human progress. They are bereft of any confidence in the worth and significance of the human prospect and become irremediable pessimists.

Skepticism has assumed many forms historically. It was first propounded in ancient Greece and Rome by Pyrrho, Carneades, Sextus Empiricus, and others. Versions of skepticism were revived in the modern period by philosophers from Descartes through Hume. In the twentieth century, it has taken on an interesting new guise as "postmodernism," expressing strong objections to humanism and the Enlightenment. There are various degrees of skepticism. One aspect of it is constructive and positive and an essential ingredient for any kind of meaningful process of inquiry. Here one has a questioning open mind and one doubts claims to truth that are unsupported by sufficient evidence and reasons. I am surely not criticizing this essential form of skepticism. But this is different from *total* negative skepticism, which denies the very possibility of objective knowledge or ethical truth. And it is this version that humanists object to, for they maintain that we *do* have reliable knowledge in many fields of scientific investigation, and it *is* possible to reach authentic ethical knowledge. Our only recourse, therefore, need not be nihilism or unmitigated pessimism.

In any case it is these two kinds of anti-humanism—transcendental theism and skeptical nihilism—that I have focused on here. The theistic anti-humanist is a purveyor of tales of other worlds, which are spun out of human imagination. The ordinary person is often prone to fantasy; he or she is apparently willing to accept the theistic parables because they provide a message of salvation that is convenient to believe in, a form of wishful thinking. So important are the promises made by prophets and seers, that they are taken as articles of faith that can be lived by and thus may become the ultimate source of motivation in life. So beguiling are these myths that countless men and women have willingly withdrawn from the active world of creative human endeavors. Theistic fantasies have become so powerful in human culture that believers seek God's grace for their children by performing rites of baptism, circumcision, confirmation, and communion, and by indoctrinating them into the Faith. Marrying their spouses, dispatching their warriors into battle, or burying their dead are done in the name of the Father, the Son, the Holy Ghost, Jesus, Mohammed, Jehovah, or Krishna. Those who are inspired by the Gospel, the Koran, or other sacred texts often seek to gain political power in order to enforce their religious creed, and they may be willing to suppress heretics and blasphemers who dare to deny it. The deeper psychosocial purpose of a *delusional system* is that it enables individuals and societies to cope with the fear of death and misfortune. Living in the hope of another world, they attempt to overcome adversity; but by exalting God, they demean men and women. "Without God," cries the believer, "we are hopeless and forlorn. We are impotent and weak, dependent on 'a Being of whom none greater can be conceived.'" The believer can find no ground for moral responsibility in human experience alone. It is only by obedience to God's commandments or spiritual guidance that we can be delivered.

Skeptical nihilists claim to be deniers of all myths. This includes the God myth. "God is dead," they affirm. "He never really lived." Using the scalpel of logic and evidence, they cut away all pretensions of divine grandeur as untrue and unintelligible nonsense. As atheists or agnostics, they can neither swallow nor accept it. But skeptical nihilists are equally critical of humanists, who in denying God, they claim, exalt Humans. There is no basis for the illusion that we can challenge the gods by aping the gods ourselves, as exemplified in the Promethean legend. Human beings do not simply follow the ways of nature. They build cultures and civilizations, but these, too, are creations of the imagination. Science, the arts, philosophy, technology—all are constructs of men and women who seek to impose their vain desires and glorified ideals on nature. But alas, all great inventions and discoveries, creations and additions to nature, nihilists say, will, in time, disappear. The most poignant expression of our existential plight are the great tombs and Pyramids of the Pharaohs. Built by prodigious human effort to withstand the sands of time, they remain as stark reminders of our intrinsic finitude. Indeed, the noble cities and fallen empires of the past are but feeble testimonials today of the men and women who built them, but who are no more. What happened to their glorious ideals and cherished hopes, now that they lie buried in the waste bin of history? "All human things are subject to decay, and when fate summons, monarchs must obey," observed Dryden.[3] The remnants of the cities of the Incas, the columns of Rome, the remains of Troy are silent witness to what awaits us all. Unlike people of ages past, we have developed the knowledge of history and the tools of archaeology to unearth and date these ancient ruins. We can disinter the mummies from their tombs, unravel the ancient burial mounds of Native Americans, or uncover a lone hunter in the Swiss Alps who was frozen in a hidden grave for 5,000 years. We can examine the primitive remains of Chinese villages, or analyze the skulls of our Neanderthal forebears. And unlike them, we are aware of the fate that awaits us all. As Edward Gibbon so aptly states: "[The] vicissitudes of fortune . . . spares neither man nor the proudest of his works . . . and buries empires and cities in a common grave."[4] There are, said Emily Brontë, "the thousand creeds that move men's hearts"—"unutterably vain" and now "worthless as withered weeds."[5]

Great military leaders, such as Alexander, Hannibal, Genghis Khan, and Napoléon, unleashed massive armies to achieve their imperial ends; whether victorious or defeated, all lie buried before the onslaught of historical time. Lenin, encased as a mummy in a tomb before the Kremlin walls, was observed by lines of shuffling Soviet citizens and idolized as a great leader; however, his reputation could not withstand the barbs of history, and he was dethroned in due time. The terror upon which he built his empire and kept his deeds secret finally exposed the leader of the Marxist-Leninist state. Glorified by Communists and hoping to build a new world, his message was eventually vanquished, and his body decays along with his ideals. The same fate awaits writers

---

3 . John Dryden, *Mac Flecknoe* (Oxford: Clarendon Press, 1924), 1.

4 . Edward Gibbon, *The Autobiography* (New York: Dutton, 1911), chapter 71.

5 . "No Coward Soul Is Mine," in Janet Gezari, ed., *Emily Jane Brontë: The Complete Poems* (London: Penguin Books, 1992).

and poets: Sophocles and Euripides, Marlowe and Shelley, Montaigne and Pushkin, Jane Austin and Mark Twain, Voltaire and Dostoevsky; and scientists: Newton and Galileo, Marie Curie and Albert Einstein, Faraday and Darwin; and political leaders revered in their time: Pericles and Augustus, Jefferson and Lincoln, Bismarck and Roosevelt, de Gaulle and Churchill. A similar fate awaits monarchs and peasants, titans of industry and ordinary laborers, the old and the young, the healthy and the handicapped, the poor and the rich.

For nihilists, all ethical values are subject to decay. They are expressions of human conceit; they have no permanent anchor in the nature of things; they have no ontological basis; they are mere exhortations of human subjectivity and cultural relativity. If no one set of human values is truer than any other, there is no hope for humanity and no solution to our existential plight. Because life is senseless and without any ultimate significance, the nihilists give up in despair, abandoning great projects, retreating into a world of indecision and doubt, supreme cynics about human pretensions. Ambrose Bierce defines a cynic as one "whose faulty vision sees things as they are, not as they ought to be."[6] This form of withering vision leaves little space for expansive hope.

No doubt I have exaggerated the extreme sense of the tragic of the nihilist who is pushed to the outer limits of the abyss—for no one can consistently live his or her life under the domination of such an attitude, as Nietzsche put it. If you stare into the abyss too long, it will appear to stare back at you. Life must go on whether we believe in eternal salvation or are aware of our ultimate finitude.

It is at this juncture that the humanist's quest for meaning and significance becomes especially relevant. The humanist asks, Is it possible to transcend the transcendental temptation? Is it possible to overcome the negative pessimism of skeptical nihilists and cynics who find all human values to rest on quicksand and who view life in the jaded light of its ultimate termination and death?

---

6. Ambrose Bierce, *The Devil's Dictionary* (New York: Hill and Wang, 1961).

Chapter 2

Courage

What response shall we make to these bipolar extremes: religious escapism and pessimistic nihilism? Is the humanist alternative viable and meaningful?

THE COURAGE TO BECOME

I submit that there is a moral virtue or excellence intrinsic to the very nature of the human condition that is at stake here, and this is basic to the humanistic outlook. The goal of human life is surely to survive; but also to flourish, that is, to fulfill our dreams and aspirations. To achieve anything, to defend our stake, or to extend our vistas requires a quality of character that is pivotal to all human enterprises. I am referring here to *courage*, the endeavor to persist, fortitude, the active will-to-endure, the achievement motive, and the stout determination to fulfill our goals and exceed our natures. The opposite of courage is failure of nerve, the tendency to cower or retreat in the face of adversity. Emily Brontë again expresses the resolve of the courageous person: "No coward soul is mine, no trembler in the world's storm-troubled sphere."[1] The human prospect thus depends on what we will or will not dare to do, how we will respond to challenges that we encounter, and how we will face death. Dylan Thomas eloquently sums up the humanistic attitude toward death: "Do not go gentle into that good night . . . Rage, rage against the dying of the light."[2]

The human species differs qualitatively from other species on this planet, which seek primarily to satisfy their instinctive needs. We differ from them on a scale of magnitude. For we are not simply passive products of natural forces, responding to impulses within our biological being, but rather interactive participants in the world about us. Other species respond to stimuli in their environment, and they seek to adapt in order to survive. We differ from them because we are builders of culture. As such, we enter into the natural, sociocultural environment, and we constantly endeavor to change it. Human evolution is not a result of blind or unconscious biological and genetic forces but a function of sociocultural factors. These enable us to intervene in nature and modify or redirect the course of evolution.

"Man is condemned," observes Jean-Paul Sartre, "to invent man," and so we constantly alter the conditions of our being. Human history is not fixed; we are not simply determined. What will be depends upon the natural order but also on contingency and what we resolve to undertake. Our transactions within nature are such that we seek objects and activities in order to satisfy our basic biological needs and desires; we build upon these by constantly creating new needs and desires. We introduce new objects into nature, and we create new worlds of cultural reality: farms and canals, roadways and dams, bridges and tunnels, governments and constitutions, industries and empires, sombreros and sonatas, mosques and museums, and computers and satellites are all products of human imagination and ingenuity. They are

---

1 . "No Coward Soul Is Mine," in Janet Gezari, ed., *Emily Jane Brontë: The Complete Poems* (London: Penguin Books, 1992).

2 . "Do Not Go Gentle into That Good Night," in Dylan Thomas, *Selected Poems* Ed. by Walford Davies (London: Everyman, 1993).

brought into being to satisfy our interests. But these cultural arti-facts in turn stimulate new desires and needs, and they take on a life of their own. Over and beyond our basic biogenic needs, complex secondary sociogenic needs emerge that intrigue and entrance us and redefine our natures.

We are surely constrained by our genetic endowment, but we are malleable within it, and we can modify and exceed it. We seek food and shelter in order to survive, and we engage in sex in or-der to reproduce. However, we also bask in the fineries of cultural existence; we develop the arts and sciences, we engage in sports and play, and we become deeply immersed in the subtle web of civilized life. Architecture and engineering, medicine and ther-apy, music and poetry, war and peace, religion and mysticism, and philosophy and mathematics may attract and consume us. Although we need nourishment in order to live, there are infinite varieties of diets, from soup to nuts, beef and potatoes, granola and tofu, macaroni and bourguignon, truffles and patisserie, wa-ter and wine. Sexual reproduction is essential for survival; never-theless, we embroider sexuality with the nuances of romance, and we delight in the diverse tapestries of taste and passion that we weave to enjoy sexual pleasures and enhance orgasm.

All of this is nourished by motivating principles in human life: the will to live and the desire to satisfy our desires, but also the persistence to fulfill our plans and projects, however unique or idiosyncratic they may become. The constant reaffirmation of our desires and interests spills out into the world. Our goals and aspirations are products of our needs and our deliberations, and they are achieved by using technological skills. The arts and sci-ences, techniques and know-how that civilizations discover are transmitted from generation to generation, and they constantly change—the wheel and wagon, horse and carriage, railway and sea vessel, and automobile and superjet provide us with im-proved means of travel. The hunter's knife or the surgeon's scal-pel enable us to perform various kinds of operations. Our world is a product of our dreams and of our determination to fulfill them.

21

Courage is essential to the human drama. It is related to creativity. Humans are capable of creating new ideas and constructs; they are able to invent and innovate. The human being is not a passive mind or soul but an active organism capable of inventive behavior, able to enter into the world and reconstruct it. Art does not make explicit what is only implicit in the womb of nature, as Aristotle thought; it brings into being new forms of reality. It transforms nature. Rube Goldberg's contraptions wonderfully illustrate the inventions that imagination is able to produce. Although we are creatures of habit, conforming to social rules and customs and stirred by instinctive passions, we are also able to conceive of new futures and to take new departures to realize them. Many conservatives resist change and abhor novelty, but the human species is by nature radical in innovation. We have created the wheel, the water paddle, and the windmill, which enable us to experience new activities; the club, arrow, ax, spear, and rifle can be used in combat; the fireplace, stove, and microwave oven to cook and bake; the harp, flute, violin, and piano to play music; the symbols, words, metaphors, and sentences for verbal and linguistic expression; the papyrus, book, printing press, telephone, television, and computer Internet to communicate with others.

The stimulus that incites all such creative actions is the affirmative expression of the human spirit. It is the will to live that is the spring of motivation, the spark of inventiveness; and it is the drive to achieve our goals, whatever they are, that is essential—whether in pursuing a love partner, amassing a fortune, winning a ball game, completing a novel, composing a symphony, erecting a bridge, achieving political power, or engaging in humanitarian efforts to help others.

Living involves many dimensions: the will to survive, the drive to succeed, and the creative urge to achieve are all present. This is as true of the religious absolutist as the pessimistic skeptic in the everyday contexts of choosing and acting. In response to the nihilist, one may say that there is no need for him to get out of bed in the morning, and he may as well turn over and die. But he does get out of bed, at the very least to write skeptical tomes and persuade others about how it is all so useless. Even a playful nihilist requires some effort.

The affirmation of courage is not simply the "courage to be," as Paul Tillich called it,[3] but the *courage to become*, because it is the latter, not the former, that is the essence of the species. Tillich affirmed the courage to persist in the face of nonbeing and death. But it is the courage to *become* that best expresses the dynamic character of human existence. Our task is not simply to survive, but to forge our own realities. We have no clearly defined essence to fulfill, only an existence to create. Humans are able to conceive or invent their own destinies. All other species have natures, which they seek to realize. Human nature is in the realm of consciousness, freedom, autonomy, and creativity. We are free to decide who we shall be, where and how we shall live.

Accordingly, the first principle of humanism is related to our lack of ontological moorings. The fact that we are free means that we must choose what we are and where we will be—within the confines, of course, of the time-space framework, and in the context of our social institutions and cultural milieu. And this is the same challenge of choice for the solitary individual pondering his or her own future, as it is for the tribe or nation-state debating how to formulate its policies.

The constant task of the human spirit is to overcome the desire to escape into another world, to continue to live in spite of adversity, to withstand the tides of fortune, to express creative acts, and to redirect our efforts in the future. This requires the expression of the courage to both persevere and to become; and what we choose to be, or where we will live, or what we will do tomorrow, the next year, or the next decade depends upon our determination and resolve. Accordingly, the *vitality of courage* is the stimulus and motivation which enables us to fulfill our interests, desires, and values, whatever they are. We have the power to be and to become, and the key question is whether we are

---

3. Paul Tillich, *The Courage to Be* (New Haven, Conn.: Yale University Press, 1952).

willing to seize the opportunities, take destiny into our own hands, and assume the responsibility for our future being.

Anti-humanistic transcendental theism is the polar opposite of humanistic freedom. For there is a collapse of courage, a failure of nerve, an escape from freedom, and a retreat from reason into the myths of consolation. Transcendentalism is unable to face the reality of human finitude. It is unable to accept the finality of death. It is an expression of human weakness. *Weltschmerz* (pessimism) gnaws at the inward marrow of the self, and fear and foreboding may overwhelm a person. Theists may be aware of the views of pessimistic nihilists that all is for naught in the end. They refuse, however, to accept this final verdict, the paradox of evil, the cruel blows of fortune; and so instead they willingly barter their freedom and reason for the myth of salvation. In an act of self-denial, they proclaim, "Verily, we are nothing without God." We are ultimately impotent, unable to fathom the universe. We passively submit to the eternal spirit in the hope of escaping from the brute onslaught of existence. We will become selfless. We will submit in prayer and obedience to the ultimate forces that we cannot fathom and do not comprehend. God, do not forsake me, we are yours, body and soul, theists plead. Perhaps the theists' response to nothingness is offered out of a love for humankind: unable to accept life's injustice and unfairness—the death of a child, the tortured suffering of an elderly person dying of an incurable cancer, the collapse of the economy, or the defeat of the army. And so theistic religion provides balm for the aching heart. It is moral poetry meant to soothe the void and the sorrow. What does it all mean? "It makes no sense without Thee, God," the believer sobs within his or her heart. An earthquake or tornado destroys a church, and a hundred people praying within on a Sunday morning are maimed or killed. Believers do not know how to interpret this, and so they redouble their supplication to God. Nature has struck a cruel blow, they cry after an earthquake, and by a convoluted logic proclaim that only God had saved them. If a prophecy fails, they may, if they lack self-confidence, only reaffirm their original commitment to the prophecy.

Courage

This makes no sense to pessimistic nihilists, who confront the same abyss but cannot take the leap of faith to overcome it. Facing nothingness, they affirm that nothing is true, that all is vanity, that human existence is meaningless, having no ultimate significance. If pushed to the consistency of their logic, if it is all senseless, they should not embark upon any long-range plans, nor seek to realize any projects, small or grand, pedestrian or noble.

Neither the theist nor the nihilist can escape from the demands of daily living. One cannot simply flee to God now nor blithely choose to exit from this life and die. In order to live, of necessity one must exert some effort and, at a minimum, exercise the courage to endure. The theist, at least, is no longer worried about death, or so he says. God is in heaven and all is well. One can exert enormous labors in the world to fulfill this religious mythology: build cathedrals, achieve secular goals, even conquer new continents, though in the end this metaphysics is based on a mistaken appraisal of the human condition and a false belief in ultimate salvation. No such saving grace is available to pessimistic nihilists.

The ontological challenge to humanism has been laid down: Can humanism, in the light of existential reality as seen by the pessimistic nihilist and in the face of human finitude, nonetheless inspire us to undertake magnificent deeds and express high idealism? Can atheists build empires, create philosophical systems, compose operas, and discover scientific theories without the illusion of immortality or God? That is, of course, the basic question to be asked of humanism. I reiterate that the first principle is *courage*, and its antithesis is fear and cowardice. How will courage be stimulated; what will be the motive to action, the inspiration to undertake plans and projects, not simply to live, but to desire to prosper and excel? It is clear that empires have been built by nonbelievers—from Greece and Rome to Renaissance city-states, Chinese and Japanese empires, to liberal and secular states of the modern world. Pointing to these facts of history may not be enough for theists who crave something *more* to sustain them and

25

something dramatic to inspire them, nor will it motivate the nihilist who abandons all dreams of empires as foolhardy.

THE INSPIRATION OF HOPE

The answer to this question is that courage means nothing in and of itself, unless it is accompanied by its fair companion *hope*. But what shall we hope for, what prospects and promises shall we seek to fulfill? If the human condition were irremediably hopeless, courage would have little attraction or appeal. The old adage: "Where there is life there's hope,"[4] takes on special significance, as does Alexander Pope's observation that "hope springs eternal in the human breast."[5] For in living, doing, desiring, and striving, our hopes are a constant stimulus to action. Hope is enmeshed with the very fabric of that which we prize and value. We wish to fulfill our goals; we strain to reach them, and our wishes are intertwined with and fueled by our hopes.

Our hopes are causative of our futures. They generate our activities and feed our passions. The future depends on what we resolve to undertake: wish is father to the fact. Living involves ongoing processes of desiring and aspiring, and it is replete with efforts exerted by us to realize our hopes. Not all of our goals can be effectively reached. Many of our hopes flounder unfulfilled; they may be dashed by things beyond our control, by impenetrable obstacles placed in our way. Yet there are always new desires to motivate us and new dreams to stimulate us to action. A mother hopes that her daughter will marry well, a father that she will become a teacher or lawyer. A student hopes for good grades in school, a general for victory in battle, a minister to be able to persuade his flock, a poet to be recognized by her peers. We thus are constantly stimulated by a plurality of wishes, desires, and hopes. Many are minor and small in scale; others loom large in ambition and scope or are grandiose and majestic in magnitude.

---

4 . John Gay, "The Sick Man and the Angel." In *Fables*, XXVII (Menston: The Scolar Press, 1969).

5 . Alexander Pope, *Essay on Man* (London: L. Gilliver, 1734), 1.

Many may only wish to bake a cake; some will aspire to conquer a continent.

Dreams, hopes, and aspirations are the stuff of which life is made. Yet both the transcendental theist and pessimistic nihilist view this life as tragic. Many have an exaggerated fear of ultimate failure and defeat. Theists in particular have a distorted sense of their own impotence. If we are all alone in a vast impersonal universe, they believe, all would be without meaning. Why strive to do *anything*, why love or forgive, seek to pacify or mollify, to create or achieve if, *in the long run*, it all leads to ultimate nonbeing? Thus, the sense of death may overwhelm the existential consciousness. Such a morbid view of the ultimate defeat of human life for both the theist and nihilist may generate an attitude of hopelessness. The mood is not unlike that of the gazelle who, stalked and finally seized by the lion, collapses in fear, resigned to its fate, waiting death in the jaws of the predator.

For theists hope is essential to the faith, but their Hope is for an eternal life. For humanists this is a false hope based on wishful thinking, unsubstantiated by evidence or reasons, a mere leap of faith to satisfy psychological cravings. For Dante, human existence is hopeless only if one is condemned to hell. *"Lasciate ogni speranza, voi ch'entrate"* ("Abandon hope, all ye who enter here") is the sign over the portico of his Inferno.[6] The skeptical pessimist shares the theist's appraisal that in a universe without divine purpose, life would be devoid of meaning. Should a person lay awake nights worrying that the sun will cool down in five billion years and that all life on earth will eventually become extinct?

CAN HUMANISM INSPIRE HOPE?

My response to this question is that *hope* should not be generalized or capitalized. There is no sense of absolute Hope shining as a beacon light for all to aspire. There is no cosmic Prospect for the human species. This is the fallacy of monotheism, which postulates God as the source of cosmic hope, a false belief in things

---

6 . Dante, *Inferno* (Boston: D.C. Heath & Co., 1909), II.

unseen. There is no metaphysical basis for hope. Like "being" or "existence," hope has no content *per se*; it should not be viewed as a purely abstract concept. Rather hope should be interpreted pluralistically. It is multifarious, of virtually infinite varieties, as diverse as the idiosyncratic values and desires that people have. Its content is psychological and sociocultural. Hope implies the expectation and anticipation that what we want will come into being. The hopes of people vary, just as their individual personalities differ. Many are as specific as, "I hope my fox terrier wins the championship at the dog show," or "I hope that it doesn't rain tomorrow and ruin my new white shoes." Or it can be socially contextualized: "We hope that our Roumanian team wins the Olympic Gold Medal," or "We hope for an early economic recovery," or "We hope for a bumper crop." Hope is always prospective, pointing to a future that we wish to eventuate, or that we work hard to bring into being: "We hope the next season will show an improvement in sales," or "We hope a great number of our students are admitted to good colleges."

Hope has both a cognitive component and an emotive basis. Hopes that are purely emotional often are capricious, as in the case of the young girl who dreams of Prince Charming sweeping her off her feet, or the couple who hopes it can afford to buy the mansion on the hill. All too often such dreams are pure expressions of wishful thinking. Thus, we should recognize the importance of a cognitive or intellectual element in formulating and framing our hopes. I say that "I hope that I will graduate from medical school next year." This is not unrealistic if it is based on an accurate appraisal of my capacities and the opportunities for success. Or I may say that "We hope to reach a negotiated settlement," as when Palestinian and Israeli delegations work hard in hammering out a peace treaty that they can live with.

Presumably our hopes are concrete and contextual: they are a function of who and what we are, where we live, and the kinds of social conditions which prevail. If I am a beggar, I may be unable to buy the things I desire. If I am deformed, the girl or boy of my dreams may not be mine, and unrequited love may ensue. If I am without musical talent, I may hope to be a great musician or a conductor, but without any realistic chance of achieving it. If I am working in the coal mines of Yorkshire in the nineteenth century, or am a coolie in China during the Fu Dynasty, my options may be severely limited. Thus, the range of human aspirations in one sense is relative to an historical epoch. If I have a debilitating disease, which confines me to a wheelchair, what I will do depends on objective constraints imposed on me. On the other hand, if I am reasonably healthy and live in a free, open, democratic, peaceful, and fairly prosperous society, I may have open horizons as a young person to become a computer scientist or a teacher, an engineer or an architect, a nurse or a business executive.

Related to hope is *power*; that is, we must have both the capacity and wherewithal to realize our goals, otherwise they are just simply dreams. Our ends depend on the means at our disposal. Some ends are purely vain and there is little or no hope of attainment, or they may not be genuine. Hopes are also a function of my freedom and of whether I am permitted the opportunity to attain my goals. If I live in a class-ridden society, my chances of improving my economic status may be severely limited by social barriers. However, our sense of power also depends on whether we have the determination and drive to seize the opportunity and change the circumstances within the social environment. In two provocative books, *Profiles of Genius* and *Profiles of Female Genius*,[7] Gene Landrum notes that innovative and creative people often face insuperable odds. He found this to be true not only about the founders of new industries, but also about great statesmen, explorers, military leaders, artists, poets, and scientific achievers— from Edison, Picasso, and Einstein to Catherine the Great, Golda Meir, and Ted Turner. Such people will not take *no* for an answer; and they will not easily accept defeat. Everyone around them may advise caution or retreat, or they may point out the hazards and the dangers of precipitous action. Yet they are willing to per-

---

7. Gene Landrum, *Profiles of Genius* (Amherst, N.Y.: Prometheus, 1993); Gene Landrum, *Profiles of Female Genius* (Amherst, N.Y.: Prometheus, 1994).

severe in spite of the nay-sayers. They have the Promethean quality of audacity and verve. They are willing to take chances.

Promethean personalities have a passionate volcanic lust to achieve. They are visionaries, possessed of prodigious energies. Often their extraordinary drive for achievement is a result of frustration, deprivation, and traumatic experiences that might dissipate or burn out other personalities. The Promethean's temperament is highly competitive and aggressive. He or she is not only a risk-taker, but also a thrill-seeker. Such a person can live with uncertainty and unpredictability and is able to tolerate novelty. He or she is often impatient and impulsive in achieving goals. According to William James, it is only by risking our persons that we live at all. Often enough our faith beforehand in an uncertified result is the only thing that makes the result come true.[8] Such individuals are highly charismatic, enthusiastic, and inspirational. They exasperate, but also motivate, those around them.

Perhaps there is a genetic and glandular difference between at least two types of individuals: those who seek comfort, security, and are fearful of change versus those who relish adventure, challenge, overcoming obstacles, and are willing to take chances. It is the latter who exert strenuous efforts to achieve grandiose goals; they become the captains of industry, the great entrepreneurs, the founders, discoverers, and creators of new ways of living, whether in the arts, the sciences, or practical life.

It is here that hope emerges as the companion of courage. For where there is a glimmer of a new frontier to be developed, the men and women of great courage will leap in boldly and fearlessly. They have the stamina and backbone to persevere. They are defiant of conventions and are inured to what others will say. They are willing to confront danger; they can bear up under great pressure. Many are daring and dauntless in their response. Unflinching, they leap forward in perilous endeavors. They are adventurers creating new worlds for us to live in. Many innovators are condemned by society as heretics or radicals; but if they do

8 . William James, *The Will to Believe and Other Essays in Popular Philosophy* (New York: Longmans, Green, 1896).

succeed, then they are heralded as the heroes or heroines of civilization. According to Emerson, "self-trust is the essence of heroism."[9] And so those who do not falter need self-confidence and self-assurance if they are to see their dreams and hopes come true. Though they may have inner doubts, they exude self-confidence and have high self-esteem. They do not allow their self-doubts or lack of self-respect to consume them. The quality of pride is a virtue for the achiever: pride in their work and a sense of satisfaction in what they are attempting to achieve; they are the titans of experiment.

Opposing them are the cowards, pusillanimous and fearful souls who are unwilling to take risks. Timorous and weak-hearted, they are suspicious of new ways of life. Lacking in self-confidence and fearful of change or seeking a life of comfort and peace, they commonly resent great achievers—those who flout the sacred cows and stand out as different. Superstition, faith, and credulity are the last recourses of the craven. They are often prey to every charlatan promising them the Absolute Truth or Ultimate Salvation. They need God, a master, or a dictator to tell them what to do, if they are to survive the challenge. They prefer the security and consolation offered by the priests, rather than the challenges of using critical intelligence. Arthur Schopenhauer once observed that if you want comfort, go to the priests; if you want truth, to the philosophers. One reason why religious civilizations have burned heretics, from Socrates to Bruno, is because nonconformists do not accept the unquestioned dogmas and beliefs of society. Nietzsche castigated Christianity because he thought it was a religion of slaves—all those who lacked the will-to-power; and he attacked socialism as an expression of the resentment of the weak against the strong, as an effort to restrain them, and as a fear of greatness. The Communist totalitarian state likewise feared initiative and dissent, and so it sought to silence Sakharov and Solzhenitsyn.

---

9. Ralph Waldo Emerson, "Self-Reliance." In *Emerson's Complete Works.* (Boston: Houghton, Mifflin and Company, [nd.]).

Courage and hope are essential to the human spirit. By the latter I mean the spirit and vitality of human beings who are willing to make their mark upon the world. Is it that I am exalting the masculine qualities of boldness and audacity? Is it the phallic symbol, the male thrust of the erect penis entering the vagina that I admire? Do I denigrate female acquiescence, passivity, and submission? No. This sexist attitude is a holdover from a bygone age of patriarchy, where women were held in bondage to men. *All* men and women, I submit, have to some extent the capacity for creativity, the verve to accept challenges, the desire to express ideals, dreams, hopes, and aspirations in the real world. Women, as well as men, if given the opportunity, can excel. What I am focusing on is the "human spirit"; and by this I do not mean some ghost-like and ethereal soul of the mystic removed from the world, but the spirited expression of our talents in the world. One can talk about a "spirited horse," meaning a valiant and courageous animal—though there is an effort by his trainer to break his will and domesticate him. There are also spirited human beings—in spite of the effort of dogmatic theists or totalitarians to dominate and tame them by tranquilizing them with metaphysical systems of false hope.

What I am presenting here is the *eupraxis* (good practice) of humanism: the virtue of courage, an emphasis on human power, a willingness to create and seize new possibilities, and the capacity to exercise freedom of choice. This is not only an ideal for rare or exceptional *übermenschen* (supermen), or the sole prerogative of privileged elites. All human beings, I submit, are able to tap their own personal potentialities to some extent. All persons have the capacity for self-reliance and the virtue of independent action. Creative heroes and heroines exemplify the highest reaches of excellence; Beethoven came from a poor family, Abe Lincoln was born in a log cabin, Mary Ann Evans (George Eliot) lived in a paternalistic and sexist Victorian social environment, Einstein became a refugee from Nazi Germany, and Richard Wright emerged from a deprived background in Mississippi.

Courage

For the humanist, Prometheus stands forth as the exemplar of the heroic figure, for he challenged the gods in their own abode. Prometheus deplored the wretched lives that humans lived. Out of love for humans, he taught them to reason and to think, and he made it possible for them to cease living in bondage and to become able to achieve a better life. It is this act of audacity expressed by the Promethean myth that the humanist admires because it heralds human power and independence. Should we seek to model ourselves after Prometheus instead of Buddha or Jesus? If we do, then confidence, the stout heart, and defiance are key human virtues—not humility and self-effacing passivity. It is the heroic virtues of the daring, unflinching, adventurous, and enterprising human being who climbs mountains because they are there, and builds castles because they fulfill his dreams. He is relentless in the pursuit of his goals.[10] We need, however, to balance courage with other values. I surely do not mean foolhardy rashness, but courage based on a rational appraisal of our goals.

Implicit in the courageous posture is the virtue of autonomy, a recognition of self-power, a need to cultivate our individual creative talents. By courage I do not mean simply the exemplary talents of the hero-warrior displayed in battle or the strenuous exertion of the Olympic champion in competition with others. These are among the highest peaks of human excellence. Rather I mean the display of the courageous qualities of vitality and affirmation in even the pedestrian activities of life. Included in this is the willingness and the ability to endure defeat. No one is entirely able to fulfill all of his desires or succeed in all of his ventures. Perhaps the greatest test of courage is to bear defeat without losing heart. The supreme test of endurance is whether we can resolve to persist and whether we are willng to undertake

---

10. The religious author and priest Richard John Neuhaus has criticized me, remarking that I was a friendly fellow but "relentless" in the defense of humanism. I was cheerful after reading that because there is an important value in relentlessly seeking to achieve your goals. Neuhaus is surely relentless in defending Christianity. Richard John Neuhaus, "The Public Square: A Continuing Survey of Religion and Public Life," *First Things: A Monthly Journal of Religion and Public Life*, no. 42 (April 1994), p. 67.

new challenges in the midst of adversity. This brings us back to hope. One cannot be courageous if our situation is totally hopeless. But is the human condition ever completely hopeless, or are there not some redeeming virtues to life still remaining?

Is there a metaphysics of hope? If we take the historical point of view, and if we recognize the finitude of our reach, is not life hopeless in the end? My answer is that it need not be, for life while lived can be good in and of itself, and the achievements that we create can have their own intrinsic worth aside from any eternal quality they may have. Where there is some hope, where the situation allows us some free choice, and where we are not completely hampered by our station and its duties, we are capable of some considered enthusiasm. Life, in spite of difficulties, still can be good; and we can find some measure of hope in our future, some worthwhile qualities of experience to enjoy. There still are some promising options. Thus, we can be sanguine if we expect that some of our goals can be achieved. Hopefully, we can uncover some redeeming virtues and some reason for a positive attitude. Indeed, under optimal conditions we may even overflow with exuberance and buoyancy, because our bright prospects augur well. Of course, in most situations a naïve optimism is inappropriate. We perhaps need a realistic appraisal of the real possibilities and some reflective evaluation of what is likely to ensue. The best course is balanced optimism. The opposite of this is undue pessimism. Is this latter attitude ever justified? Surely one must distinguish between extreme and balanced pessimism.

One must concede that sometimes a person's situation may become hopeless—as when he discovers that he has an incurable cancer and that he has only a short while to live. The best response to this is that every moment is precious; we should live it fully and still seek to savor its delicacies. Is this possible when the barbarians enter the gates, rape our women, and kill our children, or when I lose everything in a devastating earthquake or an economic collapse, or when I am awaiting imminent death? Bill Rourke,[11] a young man whom I knew, developed multiple scle-

---

11. I have changed his name to protect the privacy of his family.

rosis. He suffered for over a decade. This cruel and debilitating disease finally rendered him almost completely paralyzed. He was in constant pain. To the very last, he was at work on a book, which he hoped to finish. He could complete the book, he told me over the phone, only by dictating it to his wife. At last he died, his work incomplete, though he had strained every nerve and fiber to bring it to completion. His wife tearfully reported to me that in the last days Bill, a steadfast atheist, converted to Catholicism, the religion of his youth. A strong and committed atheist, his life had become hopeless, and out of suffering he succumbed to the myth of consolation and embraced a supernatural metaphysics of hope. There are no doubt countless others like him. But for the humanist, this is a desperate act of a despondent person who, cruelly buffeted by forces against him that he could not control and whose spirit was engulfed by the tides of fortune, finally surrendered.

Is there hope for the timorous souls of the world? Yes responds the courageous person; wherever there is a breath of life there is hope! Do not surrender your dignity as a person to the purveyors of false hope. Unfortunately, for some people, their fears overwhelm their resolve. "Cowards die many times before their deaths; the valiant never taste of death but once," observed Shakespeare in *Julius Caesar*.[12] No doubt, courage is a product of feeling as well as of belief, and the well-spring of motivation lies deep within the marrow of one's being. Alas, not everyone can stand resolute at the last moment until the end. Awaiting death, some people may finally give up the struggle. The response of a free person in such a situation is: If I am dying an incurable or painful death and there is no quality of life left, I would opt for active euthanasia and suicide. But Bill Rourke was surrounded by devout Roman Catholics who thought it was a sin for him to take his own life. And so they not only sinned against life, but also sinned against death itself. A free person should be able, like Lucius Seneca, David Hume, Arthur Schopenhauer, and Sidney

---

12. William Shakespeare, *Julius Caesar*. In *The Works of Shakespeare* (New York: Macmillan, 1905), vol. 3.

Hook advised, to determine with courage and fortitude the time and manner of one's death. This is an expression of the freedom and autonomy of the person, and it is a mark of the ultimate power of an individual.

There is no predetermined future; an individual's life is not predestined by some hidden plan of some beneficent or diabolical being. A person's destiny, to some extent, is in one's own hands, limited though it is by nature, one's genetic endowment, and the world in which one lives. A person makes choices, and consequences flow from them; our choices are conditioned by these outcomes. Nonetheless, we are free to make our own life worlds, to create our own futures, and to leave our mark upon the world. Aristotle recognized that there are tragic aspects to life that may befall a noble person who is reduced to nothing, as in *Oedipus Rex*. But this he attributed to a defect in character, which leads to a person's demise and destruction.[13] Thus, one cannot deny that there are some tragic situations in life: the sudden death of a loved one by a haphazard accident or a cruel disease, the collapse of a building, the failure of a noble enterprise, or a betrayal by a close friend in whom one has placed great confidence. Life is often impoverished not only by evil and the unexpected, but also by conflicts of goods and rights, not all of which we can fulfill or possess. There is no reason to claim, however, that life is tragic in a cosmic sense. There are little tragedies and great ones; but on the whole, the good may outweigh the bad, and life can be abundant with both. "It is a miserable state of mind to have few things to desire and many things to fear," observed Bacon.[14] It is an affirmative state of mind to find life full of opportunities, satisfactions, and excellences, the courageous person asserts. The point is that a free person has some realistic appraisal of the human condition, and he or she never abandons the human prospect because of the sorrow and defeat that is endured. These are

---

13. Aristotle, *Poetica*, in W. D. Ross, ed., *The Works of Aristotle* (Oxford: Oxford University Press, 1950–1952).

14. Francis Bacon, *Novum organum*, in E. A. Burtt, ed., *English Philosophers from Bacon to Mill* (New York: Modern Library, 1939).

mitigated by the joys of achievement. It is the courageous person who can best bear adversity in spite of it, and in response to the theist and nihilist, finds life significant and worthwhile.

I should point out that courage as a virtue in and of itself is inadequate, for one may be foolish and stupidly defend a patently false doctrine or unattainable cause. It is therefore important that one's hopes be realistic in character and that they be grounded upon a cognitive appraisal of the facts of the situation. Similarly, the expression of courage may be selfish, and people may be impervious to the effect of their actions on others. Accordingly, courage should be harmonized with a caring attitude toward other people.

Many humanistic philosophers have considered reason or rationality to be more fundamental in the lexicon of humanistic virtues than courage. Indeed, I have at times defined secular humanism primarily as "a method of inquiry," meaning that we need to submit all claims to truth to a process of evidential and rational inquiry.

Courage in one sense must precede reason. One may be intelligent or perceptive but use reason only in limited contexts, and fear may so overtake a person that he submits to a fanciful transcendental myth to "save his soul." A person may lack the courage of one's convictions and cave in to the compelling demands of religious authority. Many atheists and agnostics are afraid to come out of the closet, and so they submit to religious authority, even though they know it to be false. Thus, the courage to face the universe in the light of reason and devoid of a supernatural creator is crucial for the humanistic outlook. One may say that inasmuch as viewing reality in naturalistic terms depends upon the use of reason, the courage to face the universe for what it is and is not is a correlative virtue. Therefore, courage and reason may be said to go hand in hand as two key humanistic virtues, though the former still has a kind of priority.

Chapter 3

Cognition

THE RULES OF REASON

The centrality of reason within the historic philosophical tradition
is unmistakable. We can trace the injunction "to be rational"
back to Socrates, who exemplified the life of reason and was a
martyr to the cause of free inquiry. Other philosophers, classical
and modern, have defended the rule of reason. Aristotle thought
that "man was by nature a rational animal." Reason was so essential to the human species that it was considered its defining
characteristic. It was the highest good achievable by a person, the
source of human happiness. Philosophers have generally said
that without reason life would not be worth living. John Stuart
Mill considered intellectual pleasures to be among the highest
goods, and he observed that he would "rather be a Socrates dissatisfied, than a fool satisfied." John Dewey defended cognitive
intelligence as the guide to life. He said that the aim of education
should be the cultivation of thinking skills; the most reliable way
for governing a democratic society should be by means of the
method of pooled intelligence. Humanists have invariably prized

reason or cognition. It is a key epistemic virtue justifiable on pragmatic and ethical grounds.

This emphasis stands in sharp contrast to theistic doctrines that extol faith, love, revelation, authority, mysticism, or the will to believe as guides to absolute truth and moral righteousness. It is also in opposition to the worship of passion and power so commonly encountered in ordinary life. To simply affirm the importance of cognition in human life does not take us very far until we ascertain what is meant by reason. It is clear that the term *reason* should not be narrowly construed or limited to its use in formal logic or simple observation. Rather it should incorporate both empiricism (the appeal to observable facts and experiments) and rationalism (the use of rational inference and logical consistency). To appeal to reason, broadly interpreted, is to seek to justify one's beliefs by reference to objective criteria, that is, in the light of supporting evidence and reasons. Implicit in this is the understanding that because we live in a community, any claims to truth must be tested intersubjectively. To qualify for a fair hearing, such claims must satisfy the demand of nonfalsifiability: they should be clear enough to be understood and capable of being falsified.

It is possible to use reason so construed as our guide in evaluating claims to truth. There are practical rules of reason that a sensible person would use. Let us begin with the most noncontroversial interpretation of reason.

The first application of the rules of reason may be negatively interpreted: *We should not accept a belief as true if there is a preponderance of evidence against it, if it is found to be rationally inconsistent with other well-founded beliefs, or both.* This means that we should not cling to a belief if the grounds for it have been undermined, there is overwhelming evidence to the contrary, and it has been decisively refuted. The reasonableness of this rule of reason seems so apparent that it is difficult to know how to argue with a person who refuses to accept it. It is easy to say that such a person is irrational or has a serious cognitive defect, were it not for the fact that the tenacious effort to cling to untrue or outmoded

40

beliefs is so prevalent in human history. This is due to a variety of reasons. Many societies forbid any criticism of those traditional beliefs that are cherished or considered sacred, and this is especially true of religious, political, and moral belief systems. These are often shielded or held immune to criticism. Heretics are simply not allowed to express contrary opinions, and iconoclasts may be severely punished, exiled, or sacrificed at the altars of patriotism or fidelity. Dogmatic faith enslaves thought, and it refuses to be troubled by reflection and doubt. The skeptic Pierre Bayle observed, "It is pure illusion to think that an opinion which passes down from century to century, from generation to generation, may not be entirely false."[1] Bertrand Russell remarked: "The fact that an opinion has been widely held is no evidence that it is not utterly absurd; indeed . . . a widespread belief is more likely to be foolish than sensible."[2] Indeed, it is clear that 50 million Frenchmen (or Germans or Englishmen) can be wrong.

Efforts by orthodox religious believers to stamp out dissent are notorious in human history. The radical defenders of a newly proclaimed faith, however, may be as eager to suppress criticism as their conservative opponents whom they had toppled. Many people adhere to their systems of belief simply because they have not been exposed to the critiques of those who have found good reasons to reject them. Those who profit from the status quo are loathe to permit any form of free inquiry which might endanger their vital interests. One can think of Muslim countries, which do not brook any criticism of the Koran. The same thing was true of revolutionary communist and fascist dictatorships which, once installed, systematically denied freedom of expression and suppressed dissent. In some historical contexts, faith as tenacity is held as a virtue. "I have faith," says the extreme true believer, "because it is absurd, or contradictory, and even if it flies in the face of the evidence." To resolutely affirm one's beliefs in this

---

1. Pierre Bayle, *Pensées diverses sur la comète: édition critique avec une intro-duction et des notes* Ed. by A. Prat (Paris: Hachette, 1911–1912).

2. Bertrand Russell, *Unpopular Essays* (New York: Simon and Schuster, 1950), p. 260.

41

manner allegedly is to have scaled the highest plane of spirituality. Tertullian and Søren Kierkegaard both accepted the truth of Christianity in spite of evidence to the contrary. Many believers will cling to their beliefs because they believe God is testing their resolve—a brand of irrational courage. A similar disposition is found in committed disciples of quasi-religious secular movements and innumerable cults of unreason. Most theists of course would not accept this form of fideism, and they attempt to give reasons or evidence for their beliefs.

It is difficult to know how to argue with irrational defenders of the faith. There seems to be a perverse sort of illogic at work. Such true believers respond that they do not accept *mere* reason or evidence, or that they possess a higher truth, immune to the empirico-deductive methods of science. If they can't convince the doubters, some will resort to force to compel assent, thus overriding any reflective considerations. The defense of rational methods of science may require considerable sophistication, but to flaunt knowingly one's beliefs that are contrary to the norms of ordinary common sense is another matter. Tragic illustrations of this are the many millennial cults dedicated to end-of-the-world scenarios that do not come true. The Millerites are a classic example of true believers who persisted in their dogmatic beliefs, even after the apocalyptic prophecy was falsified.[3] David Koresh in Waco, Texas; Jim Jones in Guyana; and Marshall Applewhite, leader of "Heaven's Gate," led their devoted followers to death; they are dramatic illustrations of irrational beliefs tenaciously clung to until the bitter end.

There is nothing more terrifying to dogmatic true believers than to be threatened with the overthrow of one's cherished dogmas by a "nasty gang" of facts. True believers implore God to endow them with the strength to slay contrary facts. For the disciples of Faith,

---

3 . The followers of William Miller, known as Millerites, held that the world would come to an end in 1843 or 1844. This was based on Miller's reading of the Bible. When his prophecy did not come true on the expected date, many of his followers continued to believe in the end-days, though they extended Armageddon into the future.

the facts are irrelevant to the strength of the beliefs. Beliefs are not simply cognitive; they are not mere intellectual assertions, but deeply-seated habits of conduct infused with passions and clung to at all costs and against any opposition to them. They provide a way of life that has been inculcated by traditions. Fanatic believers, and they are legion in history, are prepared to do battle for their irrational faiths, and even die for them if necessary.

This state of mind is incomprehensible to independent thinkers who can reason things through by themselves. They are able to resist the enticements to swallow the faith unexamined. Individuals who have forfeited their autonomy to a sectarian cult and have abandoned all their critical faculties cannot exercise independence of judgment. A system of beliefs is no doubt strengthened by sharing it with others. Members of a doctrinal sect holding patently false beliefs feel more secure in sharing their fixation, and their commitment is reinforced and intensified by membership in the social group. They may consider themselves to be the children of the light, the possessors of the Truth, the blessed of God, or something else. Opposing them are the children of the darkness, the damned, the wicked, and the benighted. "True believers" in modern secular movements may consider themselves to be defenders of progress, the dialectic, patriotism, or traditional values against capitalists, drug dealers, child abusers, Satanists, liberals, leftists, chauvinists, or reactionaries, as the case may be.

Rational persons possess ideas, which they are willing to revise; dogmatists *are possessed by* ideas, which may come to control their very being. "Many men are destined to be bad reasoners," observed Voltaire, "others not to reason at all; and others to persecute those who reason well or ill."[4]

Such forms of intransigent behavior are unfortunately endemic in human history. This suggests that beliefs are not always accepted because they are *true* (though people may deceive themselves into believing that they are) but because they are *convenient or comfortable*; that is, they serve some perceived psychological,

---

4. "Destiny," in Voltaire, *A Philosophical Dictionary* (New York: Coventry House, 1932).

political, economic, or sociological purpose. Moreover, beliefs are so fused with strong emotional attitudes that they are often difficult to examine, disentangle, criticize, or reject. Many become so deeply ingrained in the social order and so fixed by custom that such persons and customs are impossible to question; to do so would mean an overthrow of the existing social institutions and the consequent threat to the vital interests of those who profit from the status quo.

If one examines the persistence of the Roman Catholic church, virtually the oldest surviving institution on earth, one sees that it is the authoritatively hierarchical structure that has endured intact, though often scathed. It is not so much the truth of its ancient revelatory creed that explains its survival, as it is the rules and regulations that persuade obedient Roman Catholics to accept its hegemony. This conduct is instilled in parochial schools and from the pulpit; it is enforced by a legion of papal officiates who are committed to the creed and wish to secure their power. Perhaps this explains the ability of the Roman Catholic hierarchy to survive in spite of abundant evidence that its basic beliefs are untrue. To question the articles of faith is not only to question Church doctrine, but also to question the entire fabric of social and cultural life that has evolved over the centuries. Can one be a Roman Catholic because of its social, moral, or aesthetic functions (as George Santayana thought), in spite of the fact that its claims are patently false? Or will demythologizing Catholic dogmas mean an end to a cherished traditional way of life, which many people may hesitate to abandon for what they perceive as the lack of a viable alternative?

On my visits to such Muslim countries as Morocco and Egypt I was struck by the fact that prayers in praise of God were intoned over loudspeakers in the public square five times a day. One can imagine how difficult it is for a person brought up in such a charged atmosphere of piety and devotion to break with the traditional faith. The subliminal conditioning of "Allah Akbar" becomes so rooted in a person's consciousness that, like air and water, it seems to engender a need. To question these beliefs is to blaspheme against the entire cultural fabric. This for many or most individuals is an insuperable obstacle to overcome.

Nevertheless, the first rule of reason is that we should not accept beliefs that are patently false or for which there is abundant evidence to the contrary; this seems to me to be eminently reasonable. Religious beliefs are usually so deeply entrenched in social and cultural institutions that it is difficult to disentangle and question them. There are other nonthreatening illustrations, however, that demonstrate the rule.

For example, how shall we deal with the following three propositions: "The earth is flat," "Blood-letting can cure illnesses," and "Trance channelers can communicate with discarnate spirits." There is very strong evidence that all three of these propositions are false. The notion that the earth is flat is an ancient conception based on Ptolemaic astronomy and biblical pronouncements. This proposition has been refuted with the alternative statement that the earth is spherical, and this is verified by astronomical observation; indeed, satellites in outer space have decisively confirmed its spherical shape. I doubt that we can take the Flat Earth Society as a serious endeavor, but if someone were to persist in the belief that the earth is flat, there is little that we can say beyond a certain point. This is similar to the proposition that blood-letting is curative, a view that at one time prevailed in the medical profession. This theory postulated that the body was full of humors and bile, which caused diseases and which needed to be expelled. With empirical clinical tests and the subsequent falsification of the theory, there is little reason to continue to support the claim. The third assertion that some people can communicate with departed spirits is equally without foundation because there is no evidence that a spirit or soul can survive the death of the body, and no rigorously controlled experiments have confirmed contact by mediums or trance channelers. Some psychical researchers may contest this latter claim, but there is a very large body of evidence to the contrary.

There is, accordingly, a second application of the rules of reason, perhaps weaker than the above; namely, *we ought not to ac-*

cept a belief as true if there is inadequate evidence and insufficient reasons to do so. By this I am referring to those beliefs which may not have been incontrovertibly refuted by contrary empirical data or logical contradiction but which still lack sufficient reliable support for their claims.

Some might say that this applies to the third illustration above, for mediums and trance channelers have claimed to be in contact with entities from the "other side." There is substantial literature containing testimony from those who claim to have seen apparitions or to have had visitations from ghosts. This evidence, I submit, is unreliable because it is anecdotal and uncorroborated by independent observers. There are also numerous efforts by psychical researchers to set up experimental seances, to witness physical manifestations in the form of table-lifting, rappings, and so forth. The field is so full of fraud and deceit that the evidence is hardly credible. One might very well argue that although the entire area has not been refuted decisively to everyone's satisfaction,[5] the evidence deduced in its favor is thus far inadequate. Moreover, the claim is predicated on a mind-body dualism that seems to be contradicted by the considerable body of evidence from the medical and biological sciences. This points to the fact that mental processes are a function of the body, not separable entities. For these reasons we may be rightly skeptical of the claim that "discarnate spirits" can contact us.

The same kind of criticism has been made about a wide range of other controversial belief systems, such as phrenology, iridology, biorhythms, and astrobiology. In many such areas, a case pro and con has been made and the doctrines of the system debated. There may be considerable evidence against a belief and insufficient evidence for it, and those evaluating the merits find

---

5 . For example, John Beloff, a psychical researcher, still defends the historical evidence for mediums. "What Is Your Counter-Explanation? A Plea to Skeptics to Think Again," in Paul Kurtz, ed., *A Skeptic's Handbook of Parapsychology* (Amherst, N.Y.: Prometheus Books, 1985). See also John Beloff, "The Skeptical Position: Is It Tenable?" *Skeptical Inquirer* 19 no. 3 (May/June 1995) and the replies to him by James Alcock, Susan Blackmore, Martin Gardner, Ray Hyman, and Paul Kurtz.

the theory or belief to be unsupported. Many people believe that the same considerations apply to religious systems of faith, not that these systems have been decisively refuted, but only that there is insufficient evidence to support their claims.

In so arguing, I am presupposing two criteria: (a) that a belief is true if, and only if, there are adequately justifying grounds to support it—beliefs are not self-evidently true but are a function of the evidence and reasons brought to bear to validate them; and (b) that the burden of proof rests with the claimant to come up with sufficient evidence and to demonstrate why it is reasonable to accept the belief.

This implies a third application of the rules of reason: *One should accept a belief only if there are objective grounds, that is, adequately justifying evidence and sufficient reasons.* For example, the following propositions: "The earth takes an elliptical orbit about the sun," "The whale populations are presently being depleted by overfishing," and "The United States is a country in North America" are all claims that a person may presumably accept as true. If asked to support the first, he can refer to the confirmed theories of modern-day physics and astronomy; regarding the second, to evidence amassed by empirical observations and statistical studies of whale sightings; and regarding the third, by referring to an Atlas, which defines countries and continents and gives their geographical locations.

An extreme skeptic might deny that any of these propositions are true for any number of philosophical reasons. There may be errors in observations; our senses are subjective and may deceive us; the truths are relative to the society in which the inquirers live; our definitions are arbitrary and may be questioned, and so forth. But these are mere quibbles; it is not presumptuous to assert that we have reliable knowledge in these areas of inquiry and that these statements are true with a high degree of probability. Of course, they may be revised in the future. It is not inconceivable, though unlikely, that Newtonian mechanics and the theory of gravitation may be modified, which might point to errors in our calculations or that a huge comet, asteroid, or meteor shower may someday deflect the orbit of the earth about the sun. The whale population might increase if Japanese and Norwegian seamen restrict their catches (this is likely). The United States might someday be conquered and absorbed by another power or even split up.

This is why it is a mistake to make absolute assertions about matters of fact (less so about purely linguistic or tautological statements that are true by definition or inference). We are fallible. Our errors may be corrected by future observations and theories. If it is unwise to make pronouncements of certitude, this does not mean that we cannot make statements so highly probable that only a fool will deny them: "The sun will rise tomorrow" and "Some oxygen intake is essential if a human being is to survive" are so apparent that we may assert them as true with a very high degree of probability.

Now one may meaningfully dispute, in many areas of inquiry, what constitutes adequate grounds for a belief. What may convince one inquirer that something is the case, will not necessarily be sufficient for another. What is adequate depends upon the context of inquiry. The reality is that the door can never be closed to ongoing inquiry. We should have an open mind and be prepared to modify our formerly established beliefs if they have been refuted or shown to lack sufficient evidence. And we should be willing to accept previously rejected beliefs if sufficient evidence and reasons have been found to support them. Beliefs should be viewed as hypotheses, judged by the evidence and modified in the light of such proof. "The man who never alters his opinion," said William Blake, "is like standing water and breeds reptiles of the mind."[6] To insist that one has the final truth is thus to slam shut the door to future inquiry.

The relationship of a belief state to knowledge is especially pertinent here. People may have beliefs about a wide range of topics and they can believe whatever they want, however ludicrous their convictions may at first appear. The question is, *Which*

---

6 . William Blake, *The Marriage of Heaven and Hell* (London: Trianon Press, 1960).

opinions are true? Beliefs may be rooted in any number of psychological dispositions. To *believe* something is to hold it to be true; that which is affirmed is thought to be genuine or real. Thus, if a person has placed credence in something, he believes that it has been certified.

But the belief may be false, and it may not convey any knowledge at all. The real question to be raised concerns the *grounds* for the belief. Beliefs may be based on cognition, feeling, emotion, desire, subjective taste, caprice, intuition, faith, speculative conjecture, custom, tradition, or authority.

I reiterate: Beliefs that we say are reliably true have been justified; they have been corroborated by independent inquirers, tested by their consequences, and they fit into a rationally coherent system of mutually consistent beliefs.[7]

There is still a fourth aspect of the rules of reason, and this is perhaps the most controversial: *If we do not have adequate or sufficient grounds for believing that something is the case, then we should suspend judgment.* In many circumstances we do have reliable knowledge, and the grounds for the belief may be so strong that we can say that we are convinced of its truth value. In other areas, we may *not* have any evidence at all, or not enough to make any kind of intelligent judgment. Bertrand Russell has wryly observed: "The most savage controversies are those about matters as to which there is no good evidence either way."[8]

In the religious domain the suspension of belief is known as *agnosticism*; it refers to those people who do not know whether God exists, and they decide to suspend judgment. The most reliable posture to take about questions for which there is insufficient evidence is that of *skepticism*. By this I do not mean negative or nihilistic skepticism, which denies that any knowledge is

---

7. I will not here enter into what constitutes the criteria for testing beliefs. I have done so in *The New Skepticism* (Amherst, N.Y.: Prometheus Books, 1992), chapter 4, and *The Transcendental Temptation*, chapters 3, 4, and 5. The best illustration is scientific method, but this is continuous with common sense.

8. Russell, *Unpopular Esays* (1950), p. 260.

possible, but the constructive and positive use of skepticism as a method of inquiry.[9]

What this means is that many questions are still open and under scrutiny, and it is premature to issue a belief either way. We may argue about the areas in which we ought to suspend judgment (as in religion) and those in which we ought not. In some cases we may suspect that one side is more likely to be true than another; but until adequate evidence has been adduced, we cannot say so either way. This is surely the case for theories introduced on the frontiers of science. In some cases we simply do not know but may only speculate. We have to be cautious that our conjectures are not interpreted as realities. A good illustration is the question, Is there intelligent life in other solar systems of the universe? It is surely not unlikely that forms of life have evolved elsewhere, and perhaps even self-conscious intelligent organisms. There are a vast number of galaxies in the universe and other planetary systems, so the possibility, indeed probability, of life existing elsewhere in the universe is not unreasonable. But until we have sufficient evidence and confirmation, we should assume the position of the skeptic about the existence of intelligent life in the universe at large.

This fourth rule of reason is especially difficult for people to adopt in actual life. For there is a desire to know, and often faith leaps in where there is insufficient evidence and where prudent skeptics are reluctant to tread. In some cases it may be urgent that we adopt a belief, as William James pointed out, because some situations in life may demand it. Beliefs lead to action, and not to act may have deleterious consequences. James may be correct about some situations, for even *not* to do something is to *do* something. In some circumstances we cannot stand aside in passive silence—even if we have no reliable knowledge, we must make a

---

9 . I should add, however, that in religion, skepticism need not lead to the neutralist position which refuses to take a stand either way. In reference to the God question, and on the basis of the evidence, it seems to me that it is so highly improbable that God exists, that I am willing to state that I am an *atheist*, though a skeptical one.

guesstimate. Here the only position is to act on the *best available evidence*, recognizing that our beliefs often may be fallible and contingent and at best only probable. Good illustrations of this are the many prognostications made by economists based on statistical indicators and the fiscal and monetary policies recommended by them—which may often turn out to be wrong.

The practical question is this: To what degree can the rules of reason, as explicated above, apply to life? Is it a pure ideal of the philosopher, impossible to follow in practical life? As I have already indicated, there are so many practical problems in being rational at all times in regard to all questions, that it is often difficult, cumbersome, or even hazardous to live by the rules of reason.

A further complication is the fact that the frontiers of knowledge are developing so rapidly and are so complex, requiring expertise in so many fields of specialization, that it is virtually impossible for anyone to know, let alone master, every field of inquiry or endeavor. We ask: Should I have my gallbladder removed? What is the cheapest and most effective method of water purification? What can I do to improve the reading ability of my children? Is vitamin C really good for my health? Clearly, no one individual in modern society has the wherewithal, the time, the money, competence, or skills to comprehend each and every field of human knowledge. To suspend beliefs for that which I do not myself have adequate evidence or sufficient reasons would mean that I would have very little knowledge about the world, for I could know nothing about subjects that are not within my competence.

The only way out of this impasse is to defer to others who are authorities in their fields—whether botany, computer technology, meteorology, pharmacology, entomology, astronomy, economics, or psychiatry. There is thus a fifth rule of reason: *I will defer to experts in many or most cases, but only if I think that they are reliable and objective,* that is, if their judgments *are based upon sufficient evidence and adequately justifying reasons, and the grounds for their judgments can be evaluated, replicated by other competent inquirers, or both.* Unfortunately, in many fields there are no qualified experts—as in palmistry or astrology—because there are no objective standards by which to reach conclusions, and there are no tested generalizations or principles to be derived from these investigations.

I am willing to defer to experts only if I believe that they are qualified; and only if other qualified inquirers can examine the grounds for their judgment and agree that these are adequately justified. Qualified experts do not reach their conclusions simply by fiat, caprice, taste, intuition, revelation, or power. The fact that they are considered authorities within their fields does not make their claims true. But if they are to be accepted as reliable, it is only because their judgments are based upon the best available evidence and reasons. Such experts also will adopt a skeptical attitude if there is insufficient evidence or reasons. The point is that they have open minds and will use rigorous methods to judge claims to truth, and these can be critically reviewed by their peers. This is why I reject theology as an authoritative field. Most theologians are *a priori* committed to the proposition that God exists, when that claim, in my judgment, has not been reliably established. Moreover, there are few, if any, objective empirical standards available for deciding which of their differing speculative claims about the nature of God are true.

In summary, the rules of reason stand as criteria that a reasonable person will understand and use to evaluate truth claims about the world. There are no doubt other practical rules that I have not enumerated. The point is that we are bombarded in modern society by a great number of conflicting claims. Some of them are trivial and some are important, and we cannot deal with them all. Where we can, we will use the rules of reason; where we don't have sufficient evidence, we will suspend judgment, draw upon the best available evidence, or defer to experts whom we believe will serve as our proxies because they use objective methods of inquiry.

In explicating the above rules of reason, I am continuing the quest of modern philosophy to find a reliable method for establishing truth claims. Historically, this endeavor has turned out to be very fruitful where it has been applied. It led in the sixteenth and seventeenth centuries to the refinements of the methods of science, and this had great success when used in the natural sciences, especially physics and astronomy. In the eighteenth and nineteenth centuries scientific methods were applied to chemistry and biology, and in the nineteenth and twentieth centuries to the psychological, social, and behavioral sciences. The applications of science to technology has had an enormous transforming impact on the globe. One can only conjecture what the application of the controlled use of scientific methods to other fields of human inquiry, as yet undeveloped, will uncover in the future.

Naysayers have constantly attempted to block scientific inquiry by insisting that some things could or should not be known; and they have defended spiritual truth, mysticism, revelation, intuition, the arts, and the humanities as providing alternative ways of knowing. Some critics maintain that reason cannot penetrate the hidden recesses of the spiritual or paranormal universe, the realm of the transcendental. The battle against Darwinism, which continues, is at times so ferocious because creationists seek to find a special place for the human species in the scheme of things. The critique of behavioral psychology continues because the "soul" is considered to be immune to scientific treatment. Many postmodernists deny that "scientific narratives" are any more reliable than other mystic narratives; and this is supported by critics of scientific methodology, such as Paul Feyerabend.[10] There is still widespread opposition to the application of cognition to normative judgments in ethics, religion, and politics. "The heart hath its reasons which reason knows not of," said Blaise Pascal. Today it is "the inward domain of consciousness" and the realm of "absolute moral judgments" that, we are all too often admonished, resist any scientific intrusion. The penultimate questions that are often raised concern the range of rationality: Are there any limits to be placed on the rules of reason? Are there areas in which it would be inappropriate or unwise for cognition to enter? Is the quest for objective methods of inquiry illusive?

10. Paul Feyerabend, *Against Method* (N.Y.: Schocken Books, 1977).

My response to these questions is that it is impossible to set *a priori* limits to free inquiry. Efforts to construct obstacles have failed historically, as scientific inquiry continues to break down barriers and to make progress. The use of rigorous methods of inquiry have been vindicated by their success in field after field. Who can say with confidence, prior to inquiry, that this, that, or something else resists understanding and cannot be known by the penetrating focus of human curiosity? The sciences continue to give us cumulative bodies of reliable knowledge as the frontiers of knowledge expand.

Perhaps some subjects are so intrinsically complex or so remote—particles on the microrealm or the distant galaxies—that we lack the brain power to unravel their codes and structures. We cannot know beforehand whether we will succeed until we try. The wisest option is to continue to probe. In any case, we cannot stop scientific inquiry. We should resist giving up in desperation or resorting to pious veneration of the mysteries.

The appeal to a transcendent, spiritual, mystical, paranormal realm is questionable, for it is postulated as true almost by definition. Why should we accept a leap of faith which injects God or Nirvana into the universe or maintains that the unknowable "spiritual realm" is beyond reason and experience? The invoking of nonnatural entities does not help us to explain what is happening in nature.

NATURALISM

The position that I am defending here is known as *naturalism*. There are at least two different interpretations of naturalism. First, it provides us with a theory of nature: It can find no evidence for a nonnaturalistic realm; hence, it denies the truth of supernaturalism, theism, or spiritualism. This theory of nature, according to Ernest Nagel,[11] affirms the primacy of matter, that is, mass and

---

11 . Ernest Nagel, "Naturalism Reconsidered," in Paul Kurtz, ed., *American Philosophy in the Twentieth Century: A Sourcebook from Pragmatism to Philosophical Analysis* (N.Y.: Macmillan, 1966).

energy or the physical and chemical structures of the world as revealed by the natural sciences. It also leaves room for pluralities of things and levels of organization and development. For this theory of naturalism, anything that we encounter and we can know is part of the natural order and is not separate from nature. The concepts and categories by which naturalism seeks to understand nature are based primarily on the sciences.

Secondly, naturalism provides us with an epistemological, that is, a methodological position. Broadly speaking, this form of naturalism argues that the best way of developing knowledge is by means of the methods analogous to those used in the sciences. It maintains that we should continue to seek natural causal explanations within the universe. Anything that comes under the scrutiny of rational comprehension lies within nature and is not outside of it. Naturalism is therefore a method of inquiry, and this entails a prescriptive recommendation that we continue to search for naturalistic explanations.

The form of naturalism that I wish to defend is *pragmatic* naturalism.[12] Under this interpretation, scientific inquiry should not be viewed as providing us with "mirrors of reality" so much as with hypotheses that work in practice. According to Richard Rorty, the core of the *pragmatic* interpretation of knowledge is that true beliefs are not "representations of the nature of things," but rather provide us with "successful rules for action."[13] Pragmatic naturalists wish to extend the methods of scientific inquiry to all aspects of nature and human experience. Rorty disagrees with this form of naturalism.

The key question often raised is whether scientific thinking and technological methodologies can be applied to the normative domain. It is alleged that science and technology can tell us about the means at our disposal and the costs and consequences of cer-

---

12 . See Paul Kurtz, *Philosophical Essays in Pragmatic Naturalism* (Amherst, N.Y.: Prometheus Books, 1990).

13 . Richard Rorty, "Pragmatism without Method," in Paul Kurtz, ed., *Sidney Hook: Philosopher of Democracy and Humanism* (Amherst, N.Y.: Prometheus Books, 1983), p. 262.

tain plans of action, but they cannot solve the question of ends, which are beyond scientific rationality. This is surely an over-statement, for scientific methods are used daily in the economic and political arenas, where computer technology, decision making, and game theory provide valuable tools for choices. Can we go beyond this to the ethical sphere, and can such judgments be considered scientific? Philosophers within the tradition of pragmatic naturalism have generally defended the use of naturalistic methods in ethics, and they have even talked about developing a "science of value and valuation." Is it a mistake to try to extend the methods of science to these domains of life?

Sidney Hook perhaps best answers this question in the affirmative. He urges us to "bring the scientific method to bear throughout culture." He maintains that "there is usually one reliable method for reaching truth about the nature of things . . . and this comes to full fruition in the methods of science."[14] Rorty has argued that this quest for a method is illegitimate, and that philosophers should abandon it as an inadmissible form of "scientism."

My reply to this criticism is that the rules of reason are themselves normative and that what is at stake is not simply ethics and politics, but science itself. Is there a justification for using scientific methodology? Yes, and the justification is two-fold: (a) it is the most effective instrument for understanding natural processes by comparison with other methods, and it can thus be vindicated pragmatically because of its fruitful consequences, and (b) it is intrinsically worthwhile for its own sake. Because human beings are curious and wish to know, it provides the best tools for unlocking the secrets of nature.

The methods of science are changing; they are not fixed or final, and they are open to correction. Moreover, the knowledge that we receive is not ultimate. It is not the perfect order or structure of reality. Verified hypotheses and theories in one sense are objectively grounded, describing what is out there as "real"; in

---

14 . Sidney Hook, "Naturalism and First Principles," in *The Quest for Being and Other Studies in Naturalism and Humanism* (N.Y.: St. Martin's Press,) 1961.

another sense knowledge is fallible, changing, probabilistic, and not perfect or absolute. We can never have final certitude.

Scientific inquiry is continuous with the methods of reasoning used in common sense. Thus, any sharp distinction between theoretical and practical judgments is overdrawn because scientific inquiry fulfills our purposes and is tested experimentally. No doubt we need a broader term, not simply "scientific method," to describe what I'm talking about. The effort to reduce all critical inquiry to the methods used in science is indeed too narrow, and Rorty is correct in considering this to be a form of "scientism." I surely do not naïvely believe that "science will save us" in any simplistic sense. Moreover, it is illegitimate to take the research model paradigm used in the sciences for *all* fields of human endeavor. We need a broader model for rationality, recognizing some diversity and plurality in scientific methods but leaving room for some continuity in methods. Do not the mathematician and the theoretical physicist share something in common with the laboratory experimentalist and the engineer? And do they not have something in common with the historian trying to describe and interpret a period in history; the lawyer arguing a case in the courtroom; the teacher attempting to get students in the classroom to learn; the politician attempting to explain his platform; the medical ethicist arguing a case for euthanasia; the football coach working out his strategy and tactics for his team to win the game; or even the philosopher attempting to wrestle with unsettling questions? Do these differences mark sharp distinctions in methods?

I submit that in each of these fields there are similar methods, and there are common forms of rationality that are used. Moreover, they are used in daily life when we seek to maintain our lawns, go shopping in the supermarket, or send our children off to school. The term *critical thinking* seems appropriate as a general model, for it demonstrates that there is a *continuity of methods* from common sense to scientific research. Critical thinking embodies both reason and experience in developing knowledge. It includes scientific research, technological applications, and technical skills; however, it also applies to ordinary life, where we frame practical judgments. And there are similar uses in ethics, politics, economics, and other fields. We are fortunate that the capacity for intelligent thought is present in human nature as part of the genetic endowment of the race. Critical thinking denotes our ability to understand and learn, to be able to solve problems and cope with new situations encountered in the environment. It is our capacity to reason abstractly, to develop knowledge, to use cognition to overcome obstacles, and to manipulate the environment for our purposes. Although some native intelligence is a prerequisite for critical thinking, cognitive skills can be cultivated and trained, otherwise they may lack focus and lie fallow and dormant. Critical thinking needs to be developed by means of education; it is critical or reflective thinking that enables us to direct our intelligence to deal with the problems that we face, whether they are abstract and theoretical or concrete and practical. Critical thinking enables us to get to the heart of a problem, to see what is at issue, and to try to resolve it. It also involves a *creative* component. In facing a problem or coping with a quandary, the seminaly inventive and insightful quality of creative thinking is present.

Critical thinking is exemplified in all fields of human endeavor. It is used by the poet who, as a craftsman, skillfully writes a sonnet, or the composer who drafts a chamber work, or even a theologian, who explicates and interprets a set of beliefs as part of a coherent system.

It is a common fallacy to regard as intelligent those people who agree with one's own point of view and to denigrate as stupid those who disagree. Both skeptics and believers are no doubt intelligent in their domains, as are fundamentalists and atheists. Scientific expertise may enable them to apply their intellectual powers to deal with a specific set of problems in narrowly confined specialties—for example, in medical practice, from otolaryngology and orthopedic surgery to oncology, obstetrics, and ophthalmology.

How do scientists in medicine differ from astrologers, chiropractors, soothsayers, or palmists? Basically, the proper use of critical thinking occurs when they seek to test beliefs by means of the rules of reason. This means that they should consider their beliefs to be *hypotheses* and evaluate them by whether they are adequately justified by the evidence, logically coherent, and tested experimentally. All claims to belief must in principle be examinable by a community of inquirers who can appraise the reasoning, replicate the tests, and corroborate the evidence.

It is important that at some point the basic presuppositions of a system of beliefs or field of inquiry be critically evaluated. For example, one may ask, Are the foundations of theology reliably established? Is revelation an adequate source of knowledge? Are the Bible or the Koran the word of God? Is there evidence for God's existence? Has God intervened in the world and revealed his purposes? If the answer to these questions is in the negative, then one should reject the entire field of theological reasoning. In evaluating astrology, one must likewise dig into its foundations: Does the time and place of birth of an individual determine his personality and his future destiny? If there is insufficient empirical evidence for the basic premises on which the claims rest, then one must be prepared to reject the whole stack of cards on which the system of beliefs rests. Unfortunately, the first principles of theistic or paranormal belief systems are not critically examined, and they are assumed to be true. From these unexamined premises, complicated systems of belief are elaborated. Efforts to vindicate them are often made by appealing to their logical coherence or historical persistence. But we may ask, Is there sufficient evidence for the basic premises themselves? If not, to paraphrase David Hume, then "commit them to the flames."

Often a scientist is reluctant to go outside of his own specialty. For example, many scientists are loathe to criticize theism, for they believe that it is beyond their competence. Many philosophers are likewise unwilling to make judgments about the reliability of a set of claims, being primarily interested, they say, in clarifying concepts rather than evaluating them. Often it is fear of the consequences to their careers or fortunes, or the collapse of courage, not the pursuit of truth, that decides the issue. Perhaps it is the humanistic *eupraxopher*—one who has a cosmic outlook based upon a integrated view of the sciences and a set of practical values concerning the good life—that is most able to provide us with some normative guidance.

WHAT IS COGNITION?

The term *cognition* is often used synonymously with *reason* or *critical thinking*. A central problem that needs to be addressed concerns the nature of cognition. This topic formerly was the exclusive domain of philosophers. Today *cognitive science*, as it is called, is an interdisciplinary field in which psychologists, computer scientists, artificial intelligence specialists, and linguists are participating. There are various senses of cognition that can be distinguished. Under the classical interpretation, the term referred to inner psychological processes—conceiving, thinking, inferring, reflecting, deliberating, learning, and understanding. In this usage cognition focused primarily upon conceptual knowledge. Today the term *cognitive* is used more broadly to include other processes of observing and perceiving as well. It is not simply concepts, but percepts that come under study. In both cases, however, concepts and percepts are often mistakenly abstracted from objects in the world. They are considered to be internalized ideas, impressions, or thoughts within the inward domain, existing virtually as two-dimensional immaterial mind-stuff.

This dualistic theory is questionable, for it divorces mind from body and both from the external world. It is more accurate to consider the human organism as transacting within fields of objects and events. In this sense cognitive processes refer to the functioning of the brain, nervous system, and sense organs, and they are connected to various kinds of behavior that spill out into a world of objects and events. This means that the verb *cognizing* precedes the noun *cognition*, and it implies an active process of organic interactions. To cognize in the active sense is to engage in the kind of behavior which is displayed both internally by conscious awareness and externally by its impact in the world. Historically the mind/body dualism led to the riddle of reality: How can we say our inner thoughts, ideas, or sensations are related to the external world? The person was locked in his inner homunculus and could not break out to the external world. The egocentric predicament seemed insoluble.

The transactional theory avoids this problem. It begins with action, behavior, and conduct. In the beginning is the *act*, and therefore a fact (f-*act*) is a function of the behavior of an organism. A fact is not a given but depends on the observations and interpretations made of what is encountered in fields of interaction. Human organisms confront a world of objects and events. Statements of facts are a result of conscious and subconscious feedback mechanisms exerted by organisms, who are able to associate objects, respond to, and interpret the world. Human organisms enter into the environment to change it. The organism thus is not a passive observer or thinker but a doer and agent, modifying the world as the scene of his actions.

The organism is capable of many other kinds of psychological and behavioral functioning. It can store information and recall it by means of memory. It is capable of conative desiring as it strives to seek, use, or consume objects (food, water, tools, and so on) for its own purposes. Humans are capable of using language, signs and symbols, and linguistic metaphors to communicate with others and thus to expand by means of knowledge its ability to cope with challenges in the environment.

Cognition in the broad sense involves a union of many higher-level functions: thinking, perceiving, recalling, desiring, planning, calculating, modifying, interpreting, imagining, considering, remembering, evaluating, judging, and so forth. Thus, cognition should not simply be identified with thought or perception, nor should it be abstracted from behavioral intervention in the world.

With the cybernetic age, great efforts have been made to create thinking machines, computers that duplicate functions of the human brain. The data can be inputted, catalogued, sorted, retrieved, and analyzed; these computers can act more rapidly than the brain. Although the human brain is a marvelous organ capable of complex tasks, computers can now outstrip it in complexity and capacity. The merger of biotechnology with robotics might make it possible to create "combots" (computerized robots) that are capable of high-level, intricate functions. These contraptions are invented to fulfill human intention. Combot functioning is analogous to human intelligence: three-dimensional multi-purposed behavioral functions of human and biotechnological systems.

In any case, our beliefs intrude into the world; they serve as instruments of behavior. They are not simply descriptions of external reality, representing what is out there; they enable us to make inferences based upon observation and prediction; and they are tested by their consequences in action. Those that are effective are more likely to be true because they are well-informed and they are grounded in knowledge of the objects and events encountered in nature.

Cognition has many functions. It can be used to describe and interpret events in the world, to compare and contrast, catalogue and classify, to unravel the causes of objects and events, or to make predictions of future events. Cognition can also be used to raise questions, solve problems, and develop skills and dexterity. It can make normative distinctions about what to do and how to do it. It can frame practical judgments, make decisions, and fulfill desires and goals. It can also be used in the arts to compose sonnets and musical works, create statues, and construct monuments. It can be used to play games, provoke laughter, and tell jokes. It is a tool of accountants and auditors. It is relied upon in communication and negotiation. It is applied in surgery and engineering, farming and fishing, manufacturing and distribution, education and legislation. In short, it provides the basic tools and materials of human civilization for coping with the world, and as such it fulfills our multifarious purposes.

ETHICAL RATIONALITY

One may ask, How does cognition relate to the ethical life? In particular, does it enable us to make rational choices?

Many theists maintain that without God "all things are permissible," for there are no constraints imposed on immorality. The humanist, it is claimed, is unable to provide a foundation for moral obligation or duty. At the other end of the spectrum stands the skeptical nihilistic, who rejects theism. Inasmuch as God does not exist, it is impossible to deduce any moral commandments from Him, with any degree of reliability. Thus, the theistic foundations of morality crumble. But the nihilist likewise castigates the humanist, who is deceived into believing that there is a rational basis for ethical choice because moral values rest, in the last analysis, upon subjective taste and caprice.

The indictments of humanism by both theists and nihilists are surely overstated. There is, I submit, a middle ground between absolutism and subjectivism. I have labeled it "objective relativism." By this I mean that although ethical values grow out of human interests and desires, whether individual or social, this does not mean that they are or need be subjective; for they are amenable to some rational criticism. Perhaps a better term to use is not *relativism*, but *relatedness*, for ethical principles, rules, values, and virtues do not exist in some abstract realm—their very content and meaning is *related* to human desires and satisfactions.

In the broadest sense, cognition evolved because it had survival value. It played a vital role in the evolutionary history of the species by enabling human organisms to cope with challenges in the environment; those individuals who were capable of critical thinking were better able to solve the problems of living. They could more successfully compete; they thus could transmit this genetic advantage by means of differential reproduction.

Various senses of cognition emerge when we analyze its role in the life of action. The logic implicit in judgments of practice is not radically different from the hypothetical and deductive methods used in the scientific quest for reliable knowledge. It simply has a different focus. If the purpose of scientific inquiry is primarily truth, that of ethics is practice. This is surely an overstatement, for science is likewise concerned with practical applications, and ethical inquiry is concerned with truth. Perhaps the difference is only in degree, not kind.

Nevertheless, the logic of judgments of practice is primarily behavioral because it is concerned with evaluating the concrete means at our disposal, and its main focus is on *praxis* or action. Practical judgments enable us to evaluate alternative courses of action and to achieve desirable results in conduct. Such rationality is prudential; it focuses on the most effective means, ends, instruments, tools, and activities likely to produce an outcome. Aristotle called this *deliberative thinking*. This process brings to bear various factors: the relative costs of alternative means used to achieve our ends, a cost-benefit analysis, the likely probability of success, a comparative weighing and balancing of possible choices, and the effectiveness of the alternative solutions proposed. This presupposes a thorough inquiry into the facts of the situation and the conditions under which action operates. It often entails a feasibility study of the limits and the opportunities available under the circumstances. This inquiry also concentrates on consequences and results, and on what may actually occur if we were to undertake one course of action rather than the next. One illustration of this judgmental process may be described as the economic model, which uses utilitarian standards by attempting to satisfy desires and optimize attainable goals within the market place. There are other models that are used in different contexts, such as game-theory strategies, which are employed in competitive situations. Are these various models of rational thinking value-neutral?

The skeptic points out that the logic of practice can be used by a saint or by a Machiavellian. Instrumental activity, says the skeptic, can fulfill humanitarian or mendacious purposes. The Nazi constructs concentration camps to liquidate millions of innocent human beings. The benefactor builds hospitals for the sick and poor. Both use prudential rationality to do so. Both may be said to be "effective planners." Albert Speer was a competent technocrat who served Hitler's Master Plan without necessarily agreeing with his final racist goals. The drug addict cleverly steals from others to slake his cravings and uses "rationality" to avoid detection.

There is a kind of internal logic of choice operating here. We can make rational choices relative to our unique situations, and we can find the most efficacious means of attaining our ends. An illustration of this is the strategic thinking of the general staffs of two opposing armies. During the American Civil War the commanders of the North and South both attempted to develop the best intelligence, using tactics and strategy to gain victory in the bloody confrontations. The same considerations apply to corporate managers who seek larger market shares and higher profits. Ford, Chrysler, GM, Honda, and Mercedes-Benz are in a never-ending struggle to survive in a highly competitive market place, and they have to use the best marketing strategies to do so. Politicians who are running for office may use rational considerations to defend their ideological programs and policies. These are often based upon their factual appraisals of the situation and includes frequent polling of public opinion and the framing of policies in the light of these surveys. They also resort to emotive appeals, logical fallacies, and rhetoric in order to persuade voters to support them.

The key ethical question is raised, How does one decide which ends are desirable? Are some intrinsically good and others inherently evil? Critics maintain that we have gone beyond purely technological questions of cost-effectiveness to the ethical *worthiness* of our ends.

Let me first point out that there is no sharp means-end dualism. There is a continuous process of activities undertaken to realize ends and vice versa. It is simply not the case that the end is selected and that this is used to justify the means. Rather, there is a mutual give-and-take such that our ends are formulated in the light of the means. Indeed, the ends are often the reciprocal product of instrumental thinking. Our means are not merely instrumental tasks adopted to achieve our ends, for they are constitutive of the ends. The means help to mold our ends by considering the probabilities of realizing them. We may "wish for the stars," but it is unlikely we will ever achieve them. Some ends are so romantically fantasized that they can never be attained. A woman may dream for a handsome suitor to sweep her off her feet, a man may fantasize about the perfect woman; both may never appear. One may have to settle for a more realistic choice of a mate. A child may wish to be a Super Bowl hero or a Nobel Laureate but may lack the talent for either. Thus, if ideal ends are not achievable by action, and if there are no practicable methods for attaining them, then they may be just idle daydreaming. Some ethical philosophers have distinguished ends-in-view that are readily within our power from remote utopian ends, which so far exceed our grasp that they are purely ideal. This is not to deny that human civilization is a product of grand visions and ambitious plans, and that if one does not have the courage to dare to dream, one will achieve few great things in life.

Nevertheless, we need to revise our ends constantly in the light of a reflective appraisal of the means at our disposal. You may conceive of a splendid palace in which to live, and you may even have an architect design it, but if you do not have the financial resources to pay for it, you are engaging in mere fantasy. Accordingly, we are constantly forced to reappraise our values and modify our ends in the light of realistic cognitive evaluations, and this is true whether our plans are minuscule or magnificent. The Don Quixotes of the world are considered impractical, foolish dreamers because they lack any sense of what is relevant in the real world. In applauding heroic figures who had the courage to fulfill their innovative dreams, it is clear that courage requires intelligence, and that the resolute individual must be equipped with the requisite critical thinking skills to bring his goals into reality.

There is a methodology for modifying our values in the light of a cognitive appraisal of the situation. We begin with the pre-existing desires, interests, and values that we cherish, often based on emotional attachments. We can examine these to see if they are fitting or appropriate in the situation. There are, as it were, webs of belief interwoven with the values to which we are committed. We can appraise the facts and conditions under which our beliefs and values function in the situation, the means at our disposal, the cost of these, and the consequences of alternative courses of action. We may decide to retain our pre-existing values or to bring into being new ones. Whatever comes out of a process of analysis can be warranted by critical inquiry. Values should be considered as hypotheses, developed by intelligent valuations, and open to revision in the light of a rational process. Cognition thus can become a *constitutive* element within the valuational process, in the sense that it can modify and recreate our values.[15]

The question that is again raised at this juncture is *which* ends or values should we choose? Are there any intrinsic values or ultimate ends that should serve as standard for any truly rational person to attain? Plato has inspired every utopian with a vision of ideal justice, perfect beauty, absolute good. He thought that reason could intuit these ideal essences and that these would serve as beacons to guide our behavior. The quest for an absolute set of ideal ends is an illusion, however. It is difficult to discover eternal essences applicable to every individual in every conceivable social situation. Karl Popper[16] has identified this as the source of the totalitarian temperament, an agenda for repressing the multiplicities of human tastes and interests and imposing a single indelible stamp on human experience.

The proper response to the question of which ends we ought to validate as "higher," I submit, is that we should allow for a *pluralistic* range. There is no single end or ends that can or should be attained by all human beings in every conceivable context of life and in every spatio-temporal slab of history. What is good, bad, right, or wrong depends on the contextual framework. This non-

---

15. See John Dewey, *Theory of Valuation* (Chicago: University of Chicago Press, 1939).

16. Karl Popper, *The Open Society and Its Enemies*, vol. 1: *The Spell of Plato* (London: Routledge & Kegan Paul, 1945, revised 1952); vol. 2: *The High Tide of Prophecy: Hegel, Marx, and the Aftermath* (London: Routledge & Kegan Paul, 1945, revised 1952).

foundational theory neither begins with first principles in the normative realm nor seeks to deduce how we should live or what we ought to do from axiomatic ultimate premises. What we ought to do or how we ought to live will vary as the individuals and societies in which they live and breathe vary. Surely, human beings share many values in common, given our common human nature and needs. I do not think it possible or desirable, however, to develop a code applicable to each and every person in every life situation.

This theory may be called *contingent* or *contextual rationality*. This means that what is reasonable is a function of the person or persons involved in the concrete situations of life. What is good or bad, right or wrong, is related to a person's own historical situation, his or her values, goods, ends, desires, talents, capabilities, social station, and duties.

This ethical theory is based upon a set of normative principles, and this no doubt presupposes a cardinal rule of the democratic society, the principle of tolerance. This is related to the right of privacy, that is, to the rule that society or the state are not to interfere with the personal lives of people unduly; they must not harm others or interfere with their rights. This, of course, applies to mature adults, not to children, and it presupposes a level of education, civilized behavior, and decency, as well as the cultivation of moral responsibility in citizens.

There are some people who reject this principle, who can't stand what other people do—even in the privacy of their own homes. They think some acts are so inherently wicked that such acts cannot be tolerated. They demand society stamp out those acts they deem to be pernicious. When you ask which ones—depending on the historical epoch—they may reply "blasphemy," "atheism," "adultery," "pornography," "homosexuality," "piety," or different manners in dress or behavior. Many disciples of puritan virtues have railed against sexual freedom or free thought, which they oppose vehemently. On the other hand, they often condone violence, or the double standards of a patriarchal society. In America, the Christian Coalition often argues in this way against liberal values. Leftists likewise have sneered at "bour-geois" values and have even attempted to root them out. I grant that the principle of tolerance and the right to privacy is condi-tioned by sociopolitical traditions and that not all societies have democratic standards. In such cases behavior which overtly defies the public morality may not be considered to be feasible or even rational.

Pluralism takes this into account. It allows flexibility in the applicability of the range of reason. The key point is that *the given* are the existing values, norms, standards of individuals, with all of their idiosyncratic tastes and needs, and of existing social and cultural institutions. In the first case, because individuals are dif-ferent, they will view the world differently; this is a function of the historical epoch in which they live. A free person, an aristo-crat, a slave in ancient Greece, a gladiator, and a general in Rome have different options and alternatives available to their contin-gent rationalities. And these differ from the options available to a medieval knight, a nomad in the desert of North Africa, a mer-chant in Amsterdam, a stock broker on Wall Street, a jazz singer in Harlem, a commissar in Beijing, or a student in Iran.

Contextual rationality is thus conditioned by the sociocultural milieu in which a person lives. It is related to who the person is, where he or she lives, and what he or she desires, needs, believes, or knows.

Individual personalities are products of their genetic ca-pacities and the natural and social environmental influences at work. The objects of their interests are a function of the amount of goods and services made available to them and the level of eco-nomic development of the period; their cultural horizons are cir-cumscribed by the artistic, philosophical, scientific, and religious attitudes that prevail. Thus, what is considered to be rational to the informed Roman senator may not necessarily be rational to the medieval theologian, the modern shopkeeper, or the post-modern yuppie. The point is that if you were born under a differ-ent sky, you would not be the same—for the influences that helped to mold your outlook vary, as do the objects available for consumption, enjoyment, and use. This can also be applied to the range of technological means and viable alternatives for you to select.

This pluralistic-situational approach to ethics begins with the recognition that we always begin in the middle of things, *in rem*, in the world as we encounter it. We need not trace back morality to abstract first principles, nor can we start over at the beginning. It is true that we often seek to discover general moral principles that may modify existing values, but we are always enmeshed in a living framework, and any realistic rationality must go on from there. There is, of course, a general methodology, and there are ethical virtues that are implicit in this. Aristotle's *Nichomachaean Ethics* was not necessarily pluralistic in the sense that I mean, yet it allowed for some relativity in application. And it was read with profit in ancient Greece and Rome, in medieval Spain and Paris, and in nineteenth- and twentieth-century England, America, and Germany. Only the content of the virtues differed, but the formal structure of the doctrine of the mean and practical wisdom pertain no matter what the milieu. Similarly, Immanuel Kant's categorical imperatives and John Stuart Mill's utilitarian standard provide some insights in framing moral judgments.

Thus, there are cognitive standards that the reflective person can apply, and these provide some objective basis for criticism and take us beyond mere subjectivism. Such ethical principles can be brought to bear in a wide range of contexts, though only in relation to an existing life world, and not abstracted from it. Critical intelligence can apply these general (not absolute) *prima facie* principles and standards of rationality.

The most general methodological normative rule for the humanist is *that we ought to use reason, wherever possible, to formulate judgments, to make choices, and to act upon them in the light of this inquiry.* This rule only lays down a general direction to take, it does not tell us *a priori* what to do in concrete situations. Only contextual inquiry can determine that.

A powerful argument in favor of rationality is as old as philosophy itself. It was first introduced by Socrates in Plato's *Re-*

public in response to a well-known Sophist, Thrasymachus who, as a moral nihilist, was skeptical of objective rational morality. Thrasymachus defended the individual who seeks the aggrandizement of personal power and who will stop at nothing to achieve his aims. For this individual the chief goal of life is to slake his desires and fulfill his ambitions. Thrasymachus argued that such an individual recognizes that it is to his self-interest to be unjust, to flout the conventions and standards of society; and he recommended boldness and determination to so act—though he observed that it is prudential to deceive people to believe that he actually was just.

Plato profoundly disagreed with Thrasymachus. Socrates argued that such an individual is at the mercy of his passions and desires. A perfectly unjust person is in conflict not only with other human beings but also with himself and his inner desires. In order to lead a life of harmony, it is essential that reason provide some guidance. Where a person's irrational impulses dominate his choices, there is likely to be misery. For Plato, the chariot of the soul is pulled by three horses: reason, ambition, and appetite. If these do not work cooperatively, the chariot will experience a tortuous road through life. Thus, reason is able to moderate our ambitions and appetites, and it enables us to integrate the three horses of the soul so that there is equilibrium and homeostasis. Plato calls this "justice of the soul."

For the skeptical nihilist, there are no moral norms discoverable by reason. Plato denied this, arguing that reason can serve as a stabilizing force and provide psychological adjustment. Aristotle also recognized the importance of the internalized role of reason. Practical reason helps to inform our states of character. It can thus become constitutive of the virtues, insofar as it allows the doctrine of the mean to provide balance. Here self-discipline, temperance, and other virtues can emerge. This presupposes that a mature state of character has developed that enables reason to function as the rudder in life, allowing deliberation to frame our choices.

Most theists lack confidence in such rationality. If wedded to a doctrine of original sin, they demean human nature. Human beings are by nature wicked and corrupt, incapable of achieving moral harmony. Only God can protect us from ourselves. The absolutist theist in ethics thus attempts to impose strict limitations on the person; the divine commandments are external; they operate by repressing passions considered sinful.

The humanist rejects this dismal view of human potentialities. Humans are capable of autonomous behavior. Reason enables us to make intelligent choices. It thus can be an effective source of harmony, so essential for the good life, by helping us to adjudicate between our conflicting desires and competing values.

Some ascetic, self-denying religious moral theorists have advised people to reduce their desires. One way to achieve peace of mind or tranquillity is by the repression of unsettling passions. This moral stance no doubt has some appeal in impoverished societies, where there are limited resources and where suffering is common. Self-denial based on a spiritual retreat from life perhaps makes some sense in those social contexts. The Stoics likewise advised a state of withdrawal from active emotional involvement because they recognized that some things are beyond our power. The wisest course was therefore to suppress inner desires to achieve imperturbability. It is difficult to turn off the spigot of desire and ambition, as these philosophies advise. For individuals who seek a life full of excitement, discovery, adventure, pleasure, and exuberance, the apostles of withdrawal have little appeal.

A further objection that has been raised concerning the theory of the virtues herein presented—particularly courage—is that not all people are capable of bold action, nor do they have the creative resourcefulness to lead autonomous lives. Is this humanist eupraxophy therefore best suited for a relatively small elite who are capable of self-fulfilling action? Do not most people seek comfort and security, and do they not prefer conformity to independence? I have argued that courage is a virtue which *all* human beings do adopt to some extent. If they are to live in the world, they need to change it to suit their interests and needs. It is, of course, a question of degree, and too many individuals give up, particularly in regard to the basic existential questions. Humanists urge them to reject transcendental escapes and to exert a courageous stance about life and death.

Similarly, some critics have objected to cognition as the guide to life. They affirm that cognitive talent is unevenly distributed, and that not all individuals are capable of rational understanding or reflective choices. I submit that some degree of critical intelligence is essential for *all* persons if they are to cope with their problems. Again, cognition is an ideal, though how it is implemented in practice will vary for individuals. The religious personality tends to de-emphasize courage and cognition; the humanist by way of difference exalts both. This is what distinguishes the ethics of humanism from otherworldly, self-denying religious systems of faith.

There is still another general consideration in favor of rationality. If we have a multiplicity of interests that we want to achieve, only reason enables us to adjudicate between our conflicting interests and to maximize our goals. A rational person recognizes that long-range goals should have priority over a person's short-range interests. This does not mean that he or she will suppress the immediacies of pleasurable experiences, only that they will be fit into a more coherent lifestyle. The rule of reason does not mean that one will root out passions or denigrate sexual desires; the burden in life for the righteous Christian was to suffer or endure them. For the humanist, pleasures, including sexual passion, are part and parcel of the good life. Wine and song, music and dance, roller coasters and parachute jumps, lullabies and poetry, philosophy and the game of Monopoly, and banquets and travel may all contribute to the good life. Cognition does not seek to thwart or dampen our exuberant desires, only to balance them. As such, cognition can itself become a psychological motivating force, fused with our attitudinal feelings.

There is yet another role for reason to play, and that is to enable one to develop one's desires and interests on the basis of a realistic appraisal of the situation. Often an individual's values are based upon cognitive dissonance, misperception, mis-apprehension, and error. For example, an intelligent concern with one's health is vital for maximizing a person's values. This means that everyone should know something about the importance of good nutrition. Similarly, if a person becomes sick, one needs to use the best state of medical science to diagnose and cure one's illness. Food fadism and hypochondria are often a result of faulty reasoning and misinformation in the domain of health. Knowl-edge is an essential instrument of desire; but it should also enable us to revise our unrealistic ends and values in the light of it.

The normative theory that I have presented is melioristic. It does not seek the absolute *best*, but it does try to ameliorate life and to maximize the *better*, on a comparative scale of values. It is not the ultimate good, but the proximate, that we seek, and this is *contingent* and *contextual*. This form of rationality can apply no matter what the sociocultural context and no matter whom the individual. This is not about what is good, bad, right, or wrong; it is primarily a methodological process for deliberating among normative values within situations and enabling us to optimize our long-range interests and desires.

Humanism surely is not value-neutral; indeed, as we have seen, there are distinctive humanist virtues. I am only discussing how the framework of "the logic of judgments of practice" (to use a term introduced by John Dewey) functions in order to demon-strate that it may operate for a wide range of individuals with dif-ferent virtues and values in varying social contexts.

There may be a problem with the above kind of rationality. An individual may be profoundly dissatisfied with his or her way of life or be disenchanted with the entire social structure in which he or she lives. The society may be so corrupt and evil that one can find few redeeming virtues. Is there some intelligent basis for criticism enabling an individual to get beyond the limits of the contextual situation? If trapped in a bad marriage and all efforts at reconciliation fail, a person may decide to get a divorce. If one has reached a dead end in one's career, a person may decide to quit the job or leave the profession. At times it may be difficult to accept the status quo or acquiesce to the contextual rationality implicit in one's society. If one is a serf in Czarist Russia or a Jew in Nazi Germany, one may be desperate to get out. A person thus wishes to reject the entire social order in which he or she is trapped, and it is surely rational to do so. Such a person may decide to abandon everything and start life anew in another city or, as was common in the nineteenth and twentieth centuries, one may decide to pluck up roots and emigrate to a foreign country, as did millions of Italians, Germans, Irishmen, Poles, Russians, and Vietnamese when they came to America, Canada, or Australia. Here one may throw aside citizenship in the old country, leave family and relatives, even abandon the native language. So it is possible to transplant oneself to a different social milieu, where there are different values, demands, and expectations. If courage is a virtue, then one must not shrink back in cowardice or fear. In such situations, one has entered an entirely new social milieu. The familiar application of rationality in such contexts may no longer seem relevant. Surely some form of cognitive knowledge is essential here if one is to manage in the new society, and some measure of means-ends reflective thinking is necessary. People on the frontiers of new continents have to adapt quickly to survive, and they cannot abandon critical thinking in the process.

Does contingent or contextual rationality apply where one does not wish to accept his or her station and duties intrinsic to the social context?

REFORMIST VERSUS RADICAL RATIONALITY

There are various options that emerge and two kinds of rationality that fit them. The first and most important may be called *reformist rationality*. Here there is some recognition that my existing life or the society in which I live, breathe, and function is in need of change. With one foot in the existing context, I may seek to alter the underlying conditions and modify the basic framework. If an individual shatters his leg, the surgeon may attempt reconstructive surgery. If a woman finds that she has gained too much weight, she may go on a diet to reduce her caloric intake and she may undertake an exercise program. If a man is an alcoholic, he may embark upon the task of altering his lifestyle and solving his drinking problem. If one expects to change one's nationality, one may have to learn a new language.

In a reformist mode a political party may embark upon a new program or platform, and it may seek to enlist voters to support its new initiative. If a society has a serious problem with unemployment, it may undertake a program to retrain the unemployed, provide insurance benefits, or stimulate the formation of new industries. If the education system has failed in a community, a Board of Education may decide to adopt a new curriculum and build new kinds of schools. Here one is still working within a contextual framework, but one modifies one's behavior, introduces new policies, and adjusts to new demands. One does not simply accept the status quo but wishes to bring into being something new.

The conservative resists change. He or she may be comfortable with the traditional frame of reference and one's own social status, and abhor reform. The conservative wishes to *conserve* what is believed to be tried and true. The liberal, on the other hand, is open to new and unorthodox policies and is often willing to *change*. The reality of social existence is that there are always new problems, new conflicts, and new demands and opportunities; accordingly we need to adapt to change and constructively guide our behavior in new directions. This methodological approach to dealing with social change at some juncture may be relatively conservative insofar as it seeks to preserve existing values and practices that it deems worthwhile. It may be liberal insofar as it wishes to liberate us from outmoded practices and undertake innovation and experimentation. The process of reform may be gradual, or it may be relatively rapid. Any new valuations may be validated by their positive consequences. As such, the contextual framework is reworked, and reason can play a formative role in the process. We may fail in our reformist endeavors, and we may have to try again and again in an effort to succeed.

Cognition

The better part of wisdom in most situations, I submit, is to combine contextual rationality and reformist rationality. Yet there may be times in life where drastic surgery is the only reliable option for a reasonable person, and here a second kind of rationality emerges that may be called *radical rationality*. One may need to regroup, restructure, or adopt *entirely new* strategies and policies.

If an individual lives in a repressive society—as a slave in the antebellum South or under the *ancien régime* in France—he or she may have as the only option an attempt to revolt, as John Brown or Georges Danton or Thomas Jefferson did, and help overthrow the regime. Surely revolutionaries and anarchists have called for the destruction of what they viewed as wicked societies. A wise person will refuse to submit one's destiny to intolerable social conditions but will strive mightily to remake them. Under certain conditions, even prudent reason may dictate radical efforts. One should adopt reformist methods first; if these fail, only radical efforts may suffice. Therefore, we may have to resort to revolution or war. This is likely to occur when we are brutally repressed. If there are truly no viable alternatives, a free person may think it better to die in valiant action rather than suffer the torture of living life on one's knees. Granted, it is far better to negotiate our differences patiently, seek peaceful compromises, and reform society, thus avoiding an all-out struggle to the death. Yet where our ends are irreconcilable and the alternative is barbarism or slavery, then a heroic person may opt for courageous radical action to secure liberation and allow for a life of decency. Here cognition may, after a full appraisal of the situation, decide that this is the only decent course of action for responsible citizens who are concerned with personal freedom or the common good.

Here we have reached the outer limits of human endurance, where reformist rationality may collapse and violence and hostility may rule the day. There is no guarantee in human history that the unthinkable will not occur. One can think of the American and French Revolutions and wars of liberation that were justified on ethical grounds. One can also empathize with the citizens of Carthage, which was destroyed by the Romans; the victims of

Hitler and Stalin; and the vast numbers of Africans who were captured and transported in slave ships to the Americas where they had to suffer terrible indignities. Human beings do endure such periods, but sometimes only the most radical efforts will liberate and enable them to realize their yearnings for justice and freedom. After a great conflagration or civil war they will have to rebuild society from the smoldering ashes of brutality and learn how to restore the conditions of contextual rationality. They must strive mightily to restore balance and sanity, bring in the arts of negotiation and compromise, and try to reason together rather than kill each other in fratricidal warfare.

Unfortunately, there have been too many cases in human history where contextual rationality has been abandoned and conflict and hatred have ruled the day. There is still another moral virtue that enables us to reach out to achieve a more peaceful and harmonious society. Thus, caring—empathy, compassion, and benevolence—needs to be recognized as a basic moral excellence in order to complete our account of humanistic virtues. It is to this topic that we now turn.

Chapter 4

Caring

I have been emphasizing the virtues of the individual who is both courageous and rational; these are among the highest attributes of humanism. Independent and resourceful persons are capable of exercising autonomy in their own lives. No longer willing to submit passively to the blind forces in nature, they go forth boldly to create new worlds, using rationality to fulfill their aspirations and achieve their goals. They will exercise contingent rationality wherever possible, and in most situations of life both contextual and reformist rationality, and they will apply the latter to social contexts in which rational thought can play a role.

It is apparent, however, that we do not exist as solitary persons floundering in private egoistic soliloquies and that the full realization of what it means to be human is in terms of *les autres*, other human persons. I can best actualize my potentialities because I can share the stores of truth, beauty, goodness, and love with others. We are inherently social animals, dependent for our very survival upon the nurturing care of other human beings. We relate to other persons throughout life in a variety of ways. Indeed, the highest flowering of the human potential in art, philosophy, and science is found in the fabric of social and cultural traditions, which makes these possible. The arts of communication by which we express our ideas and values are realized because of the development of language and culture. The mind evolves because our brain makes cognition possible and because we assume the role of others in social transactions, reacting to their experiences and thoughts; they in turn respond to ours. We imbibe the linguistic signs and symbols of our culture, and they serve as wings to carry us to wider horizons beyond the isolated self; we are not confined to our immediate spatial-temporal location. Language focuses our cognitive and perceptual powers by providing the tools of discrimination and generalization, and it enables our imagination and fantasy to soar to new heights. It is by means of social transactions that both self-consciousness and critical thinking are enhanced,[1] and it is through this process of communication that the self is more precisely defined.

It is also out of social interactions that morality emerges. In the natural world we compete with other humans for goods and services. Sociocultural normative standards emerge to regulate conduct. We learn from experience that if we are not to be destroyed in the ensuing struggle for survival, we need to establish some conditions of peace and harmony.

Human beings come to recognize that we share common interests with others and that there are elementary precepts that we have to respect, if we are to survive. It is wrong to kill or maim other persons without due cause, and we ought to care for them if they are in distress—at the very least in the small face-to-face communities of interaction. We should be truthful, sincere, honest, loyal, and dependable, and keep promises. I have catalogued the basic "common moral decencies,"[2] which have come to be recognized by most societies. These moral decencies are so essential for civilized conduct that those who transgress the cherished norms need to be called into account. Systems of law have devel-

---

1. See George Herbert Mead, *Mind, Self, and Society from the Standpoint of a Social Behaviorist* Ed. by Charles W. Morris. (Chicago: University of Chicago Press, 1956).

2. Paul Kurtz, *Forbidden Fruit*, chapter 3.

oped to protect the principles that are considered to be vital to the public good. These basic duties are deemed so important to human welfare that they have been mistakenly interpreted as sacred and divinely inspired. Human beings are prone to invest nature with their fondest hopes and values and they seek to find some kind of divine sanction for their moral codes.

From a humanistic standpoint this is an expression of the transcendental temptation. Religion no doubt had an important function historically; it provided an imperative that compelled obedience to moral rules. You will be punished by the civil authorities if you break the moral code embodied in law, and you will incur divine wrath; or conversely, if you are truly moral, divine love will be your reward. Thus, both law and religion develop systems of rewards and sanctions to insure compliance.

CARING DEFINED

Humanists are often challenged: If we dispense with the classical religious foundations for moral behavior, what will replace them? Are there naturalistic grounds for ethical conduct? My response to these questions is two-fold: First, *empathetic feeling* is the originative source of moral awareness, and second, *ethical rationality* emerges to further develop a mature sense of responsibility. In this chapter I wish to focus on the nature and source of the central moral imperative: *caring for others.*

A person may abide by the moral rules of his or her social group and outwardly conform to what is expected, but this may be motivated by fear of punishment from parents, teachers, the state, or God. Surely we cannot consider this motive for conduct to be fully moral. It is, of course, important that people not violate the moral rules, and it is especially important that courageous Prometheans respect the rights and needs of others within the community. Prometheus, according to the ancient myth, so loved humans that he wished to share with them the gifts of fire, science, and the arts. The key to moral conduct and a vital humanistic virtue is the presence of a genuine state of *caring*; by this is meant both the inward and outward expression of some moral regard for other persons. A caring person is not indifferent to what happens to others, to their interests and needs. In a limited sense, one may take care of another person, that is, minister to his or her wants—as a nurse cares for a sick patient in a hospital or a mother suckles her infant. In a broader sense, to express a caring attitude is to be interested in the well-being of some other person or persons—as, for example, a teacher helps her student to master grammar. In some cases a person may care for someone, be interested in their well-being, or be disposed favorably or sympathetic without necessarily doing anything about it overtly. I may be interested in someone's career or marriage and hope for the best, even though he or she may not be directly involved. There is a moral principle that is implicit in our discussion: *a rational person recognizes that one should care about the needs and interests of others.*

There are various aspects of *caring* that may be distinguished. The first is *compassion*. Here a person has a sympathetic awareness of another human being's distress, and a desire to help reduce or alleviate suffering. Compassion may involve some degree of pity concerning the discomfort that someone is experiencing. If a person is in pain and calls for help, I may out of compassion attempt to do what I can. For example, a missing child lost in a department store may arouse my compassion, and I will do whatever I can to help the child find its parent. The compassionate regard for other people can become the be-all and end-all of life for many persons. "If I can stop one heart from breaking, I shall not live in vain; if I can ease one life the aching, or cool one pain . . . I shall not live in vain," wrote Emily Dickinson.[3]

Compassion is rooted in empathy, a powerful stimulus to sympathetic moral awareness. The Greek root for the term is *empatheia*, which means literally *passion*. This term is derived from *empathés*, meaning *emotional*, which is a combination of *em* plus *pathos*. Insofar as I am able to read the inner experiences, desires, or thoughts of another human being, I can empathize with that person. If I can help, I do. Empathetic emotions enable us to rec-

3 . Emily Dickinson, *Poems*, I, in *The Complete Poems* (Boston: Little, Brown and Company, 1924).

82

ognize the plight of other persons and take on some of the burdens they face; kindness is aroused. In some cases, I may be able to accomplish very little or nothing at all because those who need assistance may not be within the compass of my activities. For example, I can feel compassion for the starving children of Ethiopia or the poor people of Bangladesh, and this sympathetic identification may be felt within my heart and mind. Thus, a person can have compassion yet not do anything to help. Compassion is an attitude or belief that someone is in need and a concomitant wish that the deprivation be reduced. In one sense this is *negative*; that is, I wish to mitigate the suffering of others. This applies not only to humans, but also to animals. I may have some compassion for the deer who are starving in the winter; thus, I may attempt to feed them or even attempt to thin out the herd. I may be concerned about needless pain being inflicted on animals in scientific experiments, and I may urge that experiments with animals be designed so as not to subject them to unnecessary pain. Compassion, therefore, evinces a *humane* attitude to various sentient forms of life.

There is a second sense of moral caring that is *positive*: the desire not simply to reduce the suffering but to contribute to the happiness, joy, or well-being of others. This is a form of *benevolence* whereby I wish to bestow goods on others. They may not necessarily be suffering, but they would benefit from my acts of commission. I might, for example, support the building of a beautiful public park for the common good, or the construction of a new library, or even take part in the distribution of gifts to children during the holidays. I am playing the role of the benefactor, and I may express benevolence by acts of generosity. The moral concern is to increase or enhance the treasury of goods available for a person or a community of persons, and this may involve feelings or thoughts of affectionate regard for their well-being. People who contribute to charitable organizations may do so with two goals in mind: They may contribute money to the orphans of Haiti because they have a compassionate concern for reducing human suffering, or they may contribute to a university because they have a benevolent interest in progress and think that education is worthwhile. Sometimes our deeds are done out of both motives: sympathetic compassion and benevolence—as when a person adopts a homeless child or provides college scholarships for disadvantaged youngsters.

Both compassion and benevolence, if concerned with the good of the recipient, may be said to express *altruism*. An altruistic act is *carried out for the benefit of another person (or persons) at some expense or sacrifice to myself, and without any primary expectation of reward*. It is other-regarding in its objective, seeking to reduce the suffering, or enhance the enjoyment, of other human beings.

What is the relationship of altruistic moral caring to Christianity? The New Testament has emphasized the importance of compassion as a moral virtue; this includes pity, mercy, sympathy, and a desire to reduce suffering. Christianity, however, is rooted in faith and feeling, and it is based on commandments from Jesus, who admonished us to love one another. This is no doubt an important contribution to the development of moral sensibility. It is a significant modification of the pagan virtues of classical Greek philosophy, by emphasizing a moral concern for other people.

Moral caring in humanistic terms, however, is not synonymous with this Christian virtue. First, because Christianity often takes suffering to have some intrinsic moral value, some Christians believe that we should suffer as Christ did on the Cross. Some religious extremists will flagellate themselves in the name of the Lord. St. Bernadette allegedly suffered in silence painful canker sores, never revealing her affliction to others; this sacrifice was said to be morally worthy. For the humanist, suffering is an evil that we should in principle avoid; it can be justified on some occasions for the good that it may engender. For example, if I go to a dentist, and he reports that I have a bad cavity that needs to be drilled, I may decide to suffer short-range pain for the long-range good (though I may hope that the dentist gives me Novocain to deaden the pain). Or again, a nation may suffer great hardship in time of war in the hope of gaining victory. But this does not mean that suffering or pain has intrinsic merit.

Second, ethical compassion should not be accepted as a blind outpouring of feeling unmitigated by cognition. Not all expressions of compassion are justifiable, for some forms of compassion may be misdirected or inappropriate. For example, persons on welfare may evince my compassion and induce me to provide them with benefits, though perhaps instead I should encourage them to find jobs. A person may feel some compassion for a brutal murderer who tortures little children and may wish him to be freed from prison. I can hardly have any compassion for him, given his past behavior. Thus, there are often limits to be placed on compassion, especially when it conflicts with other virtues and values.

Third, moral caring has a broader range than Christian love. It is not focused simply on the desire to reduce suffering in others; it also wishes to enhance the positive distribution of goods. Accordingly, benevolence is essential to its fulfillment, and this is focused on increasing the sum of enjoyments in this life, not suffering or deferring it to the next. Humanistic altruism is thus more full-bodied than ascetic or self-denying Christian martyrdom. An exaggerated concern for the poor and disadvantaged sometimes is a mask for resentment against the affluent and successful.

THE ROOTS OF MORAL CARING

Moral caring has a biosociogenic basis; that is, it can be derived from naturalistic foundations without the need for theological commandments. It has its roots in human nature and its fulfillment in the development of cognitive ethical rationality.

The biogenic basis grows out of biological need, and it is implicit in the long period of nurturing care that is essential for the infant and child to survive and develop. Moral concern begins with mothering care. This instinctive behavior is found in other species as well. The cat will nurse and protect its kittens, the wolf its cubs; the bird will nest, hatch, and feed its young, and teach them to fly. This is no doubt due to the protracted periods needed for raising its young. It is likely that those forms of behavior are prized for their survival value. In humans the endearment of a mother for her offspring may be expressed so strongly that she will readily sacrifice herself for them (though this may be absent in some pathological cases, such as Susan Smith who callously drowned her two sons). Similarly, a father who develops a caring attitude for his sons and daughters will work cooperatively to protect and nourish them. The same qualities may be expressed by substitute proxies, such as aunts, uncles, grandparents, sisters, and brothers, who develop consanguineous relationships with each other. Conversely, the bonds of moral affection are inculcated in children, who are expected to develop some moral interest in the well-being of their parents and relatives—to those who live in the same nest, have similar needs and desires, and develop strong bonds of attachment. Therefore, the family—whether nuclear or extended—is the originative source of moral caring. E. O. Wilson has shown that this is not unique to human societies but is found in other species as well.[4] This suggests that there is a broader sociobiological basis for moral conduct.

What may be unique in the human species—though one cannot say for sure, for there is some evidence for it in chimpanzees, for example—is that moral behavior becomes internalized and that it is reinforced by feelings of empathy. A member of the family who empathizes with his relatives is able to project what he imagines the subjective state of the other to be. He is sensitive to the feelings, thoughts, and experiences of other persons. Thus, a sympathetic response is elicited: "Why is the baby crying?" "Because she is hungry," conjectures the mother, who then feeds her. Or "She has gas," and the mother attempts to burp her. The parent is able to project his or her feelings into the child and to internalize a concern in order to relieve the distress.

A compassionate regard for the child especially comes to the forefront when the baby is sick. The parent is anxious and wishes to restore the child to health. Solicitude is expressed, and apprehension and disquietude are felt. If the child is gravely ill, the

---

4 . E. O. Wilson, *On Human Nature* (Cambridge, Mass.: Harvard University Press, 1978).

parent will worry; and if it dies, intense grief and sadness will be evoked. For a child who is ill there is watchful attention: the parent will spare no amount of time, money, and effort and will willingly make sacrifices for the child. The heart overflows with emotion. The well-being and life of the dependent other becomes as important as one's own. How many parents in witnessing a suffering child have cried out that they would gladly serve as proxy if they could, for the child's pain or death.

The relationship of the parent to the child on a day-to-day basis usually does not reach crisis proportions. Where there is no immediate pain or distress, moral caring is less intense; it may become relatively neutral in empathy, and it can engender positive goals. The attitude has benevolent dimensions. The parent wants a child to have enough to eat and to develop a healthy body. The mother or father also wants the child to enjoy all of the benefits of a good education and cultural enrichment. Parents will devote endless amounts of time teaching their children to read, write, do arithmetic, play the piano, meet and play with friends; this moral caring is carried out throughout life. Caring parents wish their children to marry well, secure good jobs, have children of their own, and enjoy themselves. Moral parents have a deep sense of satisfaction if their daughters or sons (or, in an extended sense, sisters or brothers, nephews or nieces) do well in life. This positive dimension of moral conduct involves a wish for the best for a person or persons and a hope that they can maximize the goods of life. If we love our children and wish them well, it is not necessarily because this will add to our own pleasure or power.

A cognate moral term here is the *moral caress*. To caress someone, to hug and kiss, fondle, and stroke in an endearing manner is to display feelings of affection. We can caress our children, parents, wives, husbands, even our pets. The moral caress involves an empathetic and sympathetic interest in the other person *and* a benevolent desire that the other person prosper. This involves, of course, a loving concern for the other, whom one cherishes. Parents thus may be said to love their children: indeed, they may become more important in life than anyone or anything else. "I do not love him because he is good, but because he is my little child,"[5] said the poet Tagore.

This feeling may become overbearing in some parents, especially when they deny themselves things so that their children may satisfy their needs. There are extremes, and there may be too much smothering care. Children of parents who sacrifice everything for them may never develop self-reliance. Is not the best parent one who is willing to cut the umbilical cord and at some point allow one's children to fend for themselves? The child has to learn to achieve on his or her own terms, whether or not the father or mother approves, and to become an autonomous person—a free, independent, creative Promethean.

To care for another person morally is to help that person to actualize and grow. It is the antithesis of using the other person to satisfy one's own selfish interests. Teachers who care about their students wish them to do well, and they will do whatever they can to assist students to develop. They may do so because they feel it is their duty and responsibility to do so. "One requites a teacher badly," says Nietzsche, "if one remains but a student."[6]

Intrinsic to moral caring is an internalized awareness of moral obligation. For parents to attempt to dominate their children and to consider them their possessions, a mere extension of their own values is an expression of egoistic love. If parents cannot let go, and the child is loved because he or she helps a parent satisfy his or her unfulfilled dreams and interests, then the love for the child may be parasitic. In insisting that my children remain dependent upon me, I depend on them, and I won't let go. This is the love of authoritarian personalities who do not have respect for their children as autonomous persons. Optimally, to truly care for a child as he or she becomes an adolescent, a young person, and a mature adult is to enhance that child's personal autonomy and freedom. If I care for the child, I want him or her to find his or her own way and *become on his or her own terms*. If I truly care for the

---

5 . Rabindranath Tagore, *The Crescent Moon* (London: Macmillan, 1913).

6 . Friedrich Nietzsche, *Thus Spake Zarathustra* Tr. by Thomas Common, rev. by H. James Birx (Amherst, N.Y.: Prometheus Books, 1993), I : 22 : 3.

child, I prosper if he or she prospers. Whatever my children may decide to do in life is their choice. I can offer guidance and advise them to desist; conversely, I might offer money and encouragement. But it is *their* choice. They may make mistakes, for life is not perfect. The highest kind of devotion I can extend to them is to help cultivate some measure of self-love and self-reliance. Yes, we need to love others, but loving others means that we want them not simply to want what we want, but to want what they want. In being responsive to the needs, capabilities, and limitations of others, we learn to be responsible for our own lives. Parents who are able to respond to young persons in this positive way are truly selfless, for their selves are not being imposed upon the young persons' selves. Of course, children may be immature and infantile, and if they demand and are to receive respect at some point, then they must treat their parents as persons—not simply as a source of their own selfish gratification, but as persons in their own right whom the children love and care about and wish to flourish.

There are many kinds of parents and many motives for raising children. In some parents, compassion, care, and concern may be insufficient or even lacking. Parents may be indifferent to children and even abuse or harm them. Why this is so and why moral caring is absent in some persons is a difficult question. One possible answer is that if children are abused and do not receive sufficient love and affection, they will in turn abuse their own children. They are unable to experience moral growth because they were deprived as children. Another may be that there is a genetic defect in some persons. What I am postulating is a theory of moral growth and development. A person will develop in moral stature if he or she has learned to love and be loved by others, particularly by his or her parents. Some loving concern is thus the required moral nourishment that feeds moral growth. If it is absent, the child may be emotionally abused as well as morally handicapped.

The above analysis describes and evaluates the sources of moral caring. This naturalistic account is both descriptive and normative, for some parental attitudes are considered more healthy, benevolent, and altruistic than others. Therefore, morality has its originative source in the nurturing care displayed within the parenting mode toward children and the reciprocal feelings that grow out of this relationship, then there is no need for religious foundations. Moral conduct does not have its roots in the commandments of God but in the development of internalized feelings of empathy, sympathy, compassion, and caring. Indeed, said Thackeray, "Mother is the name for God in the lips and hearts of little children."[7] Of key significance here is that in caring for other persons, we learn to transcend our own selfish interests. Insofar as the range of our concerns go beyond our own personal interests or needs to others, we are enlarged as persons. Indeed, in being sensitive to the needs and interests of others, we extend the horizons of what it means to be human. Our world is not centered on our own selfish infantile concerns, and we discover that among the highest human virtues are those of empathetic identification with others.

Incidentally, in this analysis I am not talking simply about natural birth parents, for the same bonds of affection and moral caring apply to adopted children, who once taken into the nest are loved equally as biological children. Indeed, one of the highest qualities of moral caring is precisely the ability of adults to adopt children and bring them up as their own, with the same intense feelings of moral empathy, compassion, and love.

THE EROTIC SOURCES OF CARING

There is still another biosociogenic source of moral caring. I am referring here to sexual eroticism, that is, the sexual attraction between two or more persons. There is a remarkable capacity within the species to fall in love with strangers outside the family group, tribe, or clan. One may speculate that an unconscious genetic selection process is at work. Perhaps there is some recogni-

---

7 . William Makepeace Thackeray, *Vanity Fair: A Novel without a Hero* (Oxford: Oxford University Press, 1983), chapter 37.

tion that incestuous mating may be deleterious to the race and that reproduction should take place among a wider genetic breeding stock.

Romantic love is among the most intense experiences in life. Too bad that it is too often wasted on the young, observed George Bernard Shaw, for they do not fully appreciate its full beauty and glory. To fall in love can be an overwhelming experience. All of one's attentions are fixated on the loved one, and while it continues it can be a wonderfully pleasurable experience. Alas, it does not last forever; perhaps because it is so all-consuming that we cannot continually luxuriate in it, and we require some respite from its powerful attraction. Nonetheless, how eloquent and profound the devotion of lovers. As exemplified in dramatic tales, lovers cannot bear to be separated from each other and many would willingly sacrifice themselves for the other—so intense is the love of Aïda that she is entombed in the crypt with Radames in Verdi's opera, and Tosca plunges to her death in Puccini's drama after the execution of her lover by Scarpia.

Romantic love is gradually replaced by deeper forms of affection. Like fine wine, this form of love may increase in bouquet and aroma as it ages. "With all thy faults, I love thee still,"[8] the lover confides to the person he adores. Perhaps the most important ingredient in a loving relationship is *intimacy*, the capacity for two lovers or mates to share their inner lives, their physical and psychological hopes and fears, aspirations and tragedies. Where true love is present in some degree of intimacy, genuine empathy, compassion, benevolence, and moral caring are especially strong. Two lovers are concerned about each other. They may decide to live together or get married. They may raise a family and build a home and careers together. If one partner is ill or suffers disappointment, the other empathizes; conversely, if one is happy and prosperous, so is the other.

There is a strong propensity for such love to become excessively possessive. If a person loves someone, he or she generally is unwilling to share that person's sexual favors with another.

---

8 . William Cowper, *The Task* (Philadelphia: Tower & Hogan, 1826), II.

Jealousy, hatred, even rage may be unleashed if love is unrequited or betrayed by infidelity. In other species, males will fight to the death for females, and drive out competing male contenders. One might say that in theory if one truly loves the other person, then he or she wishes the loved one to thrive and to have some independence. In practice, it is often very difficult to grant full autonomy, particularly sexual freedom, if the bonds of affection are very strong. Indeed, engaging in affairs outside the marriage may destroy the relationship and lead to bitter acrimony and divorce. But one may ask, If a person wishes his children to actualize themselves, why not husbands, wives, and lovers?

Some sexologists have recommended that partners should develop more compassionate and tolerant relationships, even open-ended marital arrangements. They recognize that dependent parasitical love has too long dominated women and kept them subservient to men. Should not women have equal rights with men and the same opportunities to realize their potentialities? Thus, a truly moral marriage would be one in which there is respect for autonomy and diversity, and some measure of freedom. One must, however, exert care that the trust of the other person is not betrayed and that the fidelity to each other is not so undermined that a viable marriage is no longer possible. It is possible for many human beings to enter into loving relationships of different levels with several persons. Monogamy has some merit, especially where two people are compatible and congenial throughout a long life, but it is not necessarily the sole criterion for all relationships. Two people may not be compatible with each other throughout a lifetime, they may become bored, grow tired of each other, and seek other relationships and other persons to love. Pluralistic relationships and affairs may thus develop. A strong case can be made, however, for monogamous relationships. Trust and fidelity bring deeper values, and commitment and devotion encourage lasting bonds of moral affection that cannot and should not be compromised.

Loving relationships need not be solely heterosexual. Homosexual or lesbian relationships can be as intense as heterosexual ones. Indeed, such relationships may require even greater efforts to keep them viable. Why is this so? Is it because there is a great divide—whether biological or social—that has to be bridged? To be able to overcome these boundaries is remarkable; though for some, homosexuality is as natural as heterosexuality. If the predisposition for it is genetic in origin, as seems likely, then to provide some release for two same-sex partners can be a source of intense fulfillment. Where there is a truly caring relationship between two people of the same gender, new moral bonds can emerge that can be as compelling as in heterosexual relationships. These unions involve both sexual and moral components, and when they are infused with moral caring and the moral caress, they can prosper.

FRIENDSHIP

We now take an important leap beyond the family and beyond the sexual reproductive unit, which are both essential for the survival of the species, to another plane—the development of friendships. Many kinds of moral collegiality emerge in such relationships, and they exemplify new dimensions of moral caring. The capacity for friendship marks a pivotal turning point of moral caring outside of one's consanguineous clan. I am not referring to the moral relationships between brothers, sisters, and other relatives within the extended family, but to the development of new bonds of friendship between strangers. This is illustrated by the interdependence and affection that can develop between comrades in arms or between total strangers who come together for short periods in life. We develop relationships with fellow students in the same class or school, or co-workers in the same factory, or with neighbors living on the same street or in the same town. These friendly relationships may become long-standing and involve many forms of cooperative activity. Friends may work, play, or dine together, meet in church socials, in clubs or cafés. The point is that we get to know other people, some casually, some deeply, and they become persons whom we cherish. A true friend is one in whom we can confide, reveal our inner secrets, count on in times of need and sorrow, and enjoy in times of laughter and delight. In a meaningful friendship, our caring is mutual. We relish each other's company. We respect and admire each other's growth and actualization.

Indeed, perhaps the most eloquent display of moral concern—compassion and benevolence, empathy and generosity—is between friends, who are neither members of the same family nor sexual partners. The voluntary willingness to do a good deed or to make a sacrifice for a friend and to genuinely wish him or her success on his or her own terms is among the highest exemplification of the qualities of moral excellence. It is also a test case of self-interest versus altruistic theories. To consider a friend merely a friend because of self-interest—what he or she can do for me, and not out of a genuine moral concern for the other person intrinsically, is to betray the essence of friendship. Granted, there are friendly relationships based on convenience that may develop between two colleagues in the same office or two bankers involved in a deal and doing each other a favor, for example; but this does not characterize the full quality of friendship, which in its noblest expression is a *moral* relationship. Clearly, it is usually not a question of either/or, and many friendly relationships are based upon *both* convenience and a moral bond.[9]

ALTRUISM

Are acts of compassion and benevolence a genuine expression of altruistic concern, done without any hope of personal gain; or are they motivated ultimately for selfish purposes? A person may contribute to a charity because he will receive a tax deduction or public acclaim. If so, the motive may be primarily self-interest. Another person, however, may do so principally for the benefit of others, without any expectation of recognition or reward; he may not even request a tax deduction and may contribute anony-

---

9 . For a fuller discussion of friendships, see my books *Forbidden Fruit*, chapter 5; and *Exuberance*, chapter 7.

mously. One may ask: Are *any* acts truly altruistic, or is there an element of self-deception here?

The cynic denies that any acts are purely altruistic in intention, and he endeavors to reduce all such acts to egoism. At this point a theory of psychological motivation becomes relevant. A utilitarian might argue that the motive of an act is irrelevant to its moral quality. The important factors are the consequences to the general welfare, the increase in the sum of pleasure or happiness, and the reduction of pain or unhappiness. There may be some truth to this appraisal. It is not what you say or feel, but what you *do* that counts. This issue, however, is of vital significance to humanism and its conception of human nature. It does matter to us whether the milk of human kindness and the spirit of generosity are genuine and whether human beings are capable of other-regarding compassionate and benevolent caring.

Many theists hold a bleak view of human nature; the doctrine of original sin demeans who we are. Are humans corrupt, brutal, evil, and interested only in satisfying their own selfish desires—as the pessimistic nihilist claims? Or do they have the potentiality for real moral caring? Without being accused of naïve optimism and an unrealistic appraisal of the human condition, I submit that there are wholesome moral dimensions intrinsic to the human species—at least potentially—and that these can be nourished so that they reach fruition.

The theist denies that human beings are capable of such autonomous moral behavior. Only God can redeem man from evil; humans are impotent to save themselves. If this dismal view is mistaken and human beings are capable of empathy, compassion, and benevolence without the sanctions and admonitions of deity or without motives of pure self-interest, then we *can* do something about enhancing the ethical dimensions of life. Whether any human being will be moved by altruistic moral caring is a complex question; it depends on the social and cultural environment in which he or she lives, the educational influences, and the rewards and inducements offered. No doubt we do things for a variety of motives, and these include not only self-interest and altruism, but also a whole host of other complex causes. The challenge to the humanist is whether altruistic motivation is *intrinsic* to our very nature—at least potentially—and whether men and women can mitigate the evils that beset them in the world and redeem themselves. Conversely, the challenge is whether they have to barter their souls for false doctrines of salvation if they are to behave morally. To argue, as the humanist has, that moral impulses and imperatives are intrinsic to the human being requires us to examine their sources in human behavior; and by doing so we have found a naturalistic ground for moral conscience.

Egoism and altruism are both partially true; they are false only if either is taken as a comprehensive theory of motivation. Extreme self-interest theories attempt to reduce all human motives to a single source: the selfish desire for pleasure, sexual gratification, power, glory, or gain. Self-interest clearly applies to patently self-motivated actions undertaken to reduce a person's needs or to satisfy his desires. But does it apply universally to any and all acts, including those that appear to be other-regarding, charitable, or self-sacrificing? An organism surely needs to engage in self-interested forms of behavior if it is to survive and function. It needs to satisfy its hunger for food, protect itself from danger, and seek sexual gratification. Thus, self-interest is a necessary component of any person's life; it can be justified rationally. But the issue is whether *all* motives are self-centered. I think the error lies in the failure to ascertain if the *primary* object of desire is one's own gratification or that of others, for there is a basic difference in the objective or goal of an act. Benevolent acts have *other* persons' interests in mind. In many acts the agent's own interest is involved, but the agent may also be interested in helping others—so there can be a double focus. Surely we should not blur all distinctions and claim that the motivation of a self-seeking hedonist or power-hungry despot is the *same as* an other-regarding parent, educator or humanitarian who genuinely wishes to devote himself or herself to enhancing the welfare of others.

Conversely, the egoist has a valid case to make against altruists who seek to smother creative initiative, courageous independence, or individuality, and extol self-effacing sacrifice as the highest virtue. Antony Flew[10] protests vehemently against the efforts by socialists and welfare liberals to use the state to impose forms of egalitarianism on society. This can dampen individual initiative, he claims, which is the spark of human creativity. The egoist thus has a right to object to the effort by communitarians to condemn all self-centered behavior as evil. The common good is perhaps best fulfilled by maximizing individual freedom, not supressing it, thus allowing incentive and enterprise to increase the sum of wealth for society. Promethean courage can likewise be destroyed by the legions of God's disciples imposing their standards of self-sacrifice in the name of compassion as the highest virtue, thereby demeaning courage, independence, and self-determination. Libertarians reject the morbid Augustinian-Christian view that anything done out of self-interest (including the satisfaction of erotic impulses) is venal and wicked.

This should not, however, deny the capacity for genuine altruistic loving, caring behavior in the human being and the need for communitarian cooperative acts. I submit that there is a need to receive love but also to give it; this is not only the desire to be at the center of affection (an infantile response in itself), but also the need to extend it to others. It is this capacity to bestow love and affection, and to be compassionate and benevolent that expresses among the highest qualities of human morality. The salient point, however, is that there is no contradiction in recognizing that we are *both* self-centered, as we should be, *and* altruistic, which is necessary if we are to live and work together in communities. It is the capacity for altruistic behavior that is crucial to the humanistic eupraxophy. We need to encourage good Samaritans to appreciate the biblical injunction, "Thou shalt love thy neighbor as thyself." We need to extend the range of our moral concern to the aliens in our midst and beyond our borders. But to what extent is

---

10. Antony Flew, *The Politics of Procrustes* (Amherst, N.Y.: Prometheus Books, 1981).

this possible, given history's testimony of the capacity of human beings to be cruel and rapacious, particularly toward those outside of one's community?

Critics maintain that humanism's positive appraisal of human nature is too high; they remonstrate that mankind is incredibly selfish and vindictive. The greatest enemy to man, states the cynic, is man. Robert Burton observed that man is like Aesop's fox who, "when he had lost his tail, would have all his fellow-foxes cut off theirs."[11] William James maintained that "Man, biologically considered . . . is the most formidable of all the beasts of prey . . . and indeed, the only one that preys systematically on its own species."[12] The lessons from history about the dark side of human behavior should disabuse us of any simplistic romantic ideals about the beneficent nature of human beings. There is a reoccurring saga of men and women brutalizing those who are different from them. Once a person is reduced to an inferior status, by denigration of his or her race, gender, ethnic or national origin, or class, it is easier to violate his or her moral dignity.

The causes for such cruelty are complex, and they have many sources in our nature and in society. These are rooted no doubt in the fact that we were at one time uncivilized wild beasts, ferocious and cunning, capable of killing and destroying those who were viewed as antagonists. Our capacity to kill is demonstrated in our relationships to other animals, which we are ready and able to hunt, track, kill and eat, and to use their skin for warmth and protection. We have domesticated some animals and used them as beasts of burden, working them to their capacity. But humans are also capable of extending the range of moral concern to animals within their own circle and to express care, love, and affection for their dogs, cats, cows, sheep, and horses. We express a complex set of attitudes and motives to animals. Some people

---

11 . Robert Burton, *Anatomy of Melancholy: What It Is, with All the Kinds, Causes, Symptoms, Prognostics, and Several Cures of It* (Boston: William Veazie, 1859).

12 . William James, *Memories and Studies* (New York: Longmans, Green, 1911).

are vegetarian and will not kill or eat animals. Many feel strongly about defending animal rights. Thus, our relationship to other animal species is ambivalent: we can demonstrate hate and fear or love and affection.

The issue here concerns our relationship to other human beings. It is likewise bipolar, for we are capable of displaying either cruelty or kindness, hatred or generosity. These impulses, no doubt rooted in our evolutionary past, emerged as part of our struggle for survival. Humans are born as naked apes. The entire moral history of the race has to be instilled in every youngster from the moment of birth; each of us is only one generation away from savagery.

Our capacity for cruelty to other humans has many sources; among the most important are the *instinct for aggression*, the *territorial imperative*, and the proclivity for ethnic tribalism and hatred.

The *instinct for aggression* has been postulated by the behavioral physiologist Konrad Lorenz.[13] Lorenz maintained that aggression is found in many species, including the human species. This theory is highly controversial, though it seems to me to have some merit, perhaps not as an instinct but as a *tendency*. There are a number of basic drives that such species commonly display: feeding, reproduction, flight, and aggression. Aggression, which occurs particularly between males, has been called the "fighting or killer instinct" because it is directed ferociously against members of the same species. The discharge of aggression between males is primarily in the battle for females. We can see this with other animals, such as chimpanzees, reindeer, and buffalo. The strongest and the most wily male is able to defeat other males and to gain by sheer power the right to reproduce. This tendency in the evolutionary process apparently ensures that the strongest and healthiest will survive and transmit their genes to their offspring. This struggle can become vicious in intensity. Implicit is a tendency for some males to impose by force their sexual desires on females. It is largely by means of the restraints of civilization

---

13 . Konrad Lorenz, *On Aggression* (New York: Harcourt, Brace and World, 1966).

and by developing a moral sense that this tendency has been moderated or curbed in the human species.

The *territorial imperative* is another tendency that goads some members of a species to guard their own territory. Some animals will mark their territory with urinary odor and threaten anyone who seeks to violate their turf. Dogs will bark to ward off invaders of its territory and humans will fight to protect their land. Terrible wars have been waged to secure one's soil.

Human beings tend to congregate in breeding groups, clans, or tribes. This leads to the development of isolated, genetically distinct racial and ethnic stocks. There are constant conflicts between diverse groups, and warlike aggression between them is an ongoing feature of human history. Often in such encounters moral standards are forgotten. Some animals, such as rats, are paragons of social virtue to members of their own breeding pack or social organization, but they are transformed into venomous brutes when they encounter members of other packs or social organizations of the same species; they will fight them until the death. Regrettably, similar behavior is displayed in human collectivities, and the most bestial wars of extinction have been against foreigners, outsiders, aliens, even those living in nearby localities.

Paradoxically, wars of extermination are even fought between groups of people who may be of similar stock or cultural heritage yet differ only in some minor manner or trait. Religious differences are a source of intense hatred. The Jews have often been hated in the lands in which they have sojourned. Muslims, Hindus, Catholics, Protestants, and other religious sects have engaged in ferocious wars—usually in the name of God or some higher religious dogma. Similarly, antagonisms apply to people of different racial characteristics, and bloody wars have been fought on the grounds of racial or ethnic purity. Discriminatory distinctions can be made on the basis of language or culture, as the splits between the French and Walloon populations of Belgium or the Francophones and Anglophones of Canada demonstrate. Hostility may be based on caste systems, as with the un-

100

touchables in India. Or it may be based on economic and class distinctions, as with aristocratic and bourgeois discrimination against the "undeserving poor" or left-wing attacks on the "plutocratic malefactors of great wealth."

These deep-seated animosities toward members of different groups are rooted in a great number of other human drives. All too common in human history are the seeds of resentment, envy, or jealousy, the lust for power, the greed for wealth, the passion for fame and glory, and the tendency toward laziness or sloth. All of these may stimulate self-seeking gratification at the expense of moral caring.

Whatever the complex psychobiological and sociocultural causes of human antagonisms, the central question is whether the scope of moral caring can be extended, and if so, how far? There is little doubt that the common moral decencies within the group help to socialize and tame the naked ape. Can these moral norms be broadened beyond the inner group so that they apply to human beings outside the range of intercourse? The great challenge to morality is whether the compass of moral caring can be universalized so that it applies to *all* human beings. Can our sensitivity to the needs of others be made more extensive, and if so, how do we enlarge the boundaries of moral caring?

Let us return to the original question raised above. If human beings are capable of both good and evil, what can be done to ensure the realization of their positive moral potentialities? This is a complex question. Its solution, I submit, depends upon ensuring favorable social and cultural conditions that will make this possible. This means, first, that we will use education as a primary means for realizing moral growth and development; and second, that we will support legislation for developing open democratic institutions in societies, which will allow some measure of individual freedom and autonomy and some respect for human rights.

It should be conceded that some individuals may be beyond the pale, incapable of moral caring. Some individuals are or have become so rapacious, sadistic, cruel, or immoral that there is no hope of modifying their behavior. One can think of moral monsters who prey on the innocent—Caligula, Hitler, and Stalin, or such serial killers as Ted Bundy and Jeffrey Dahmer, human beings capable of committing the most heinous crimes. Perhaps these sociopaths are deficient because of some chromosomal defect. Much the same as some individuals are color-blind, they may be morally blind, incapable of moral empathy. Some theorists have speculated that such behavior is abnormal and may be caused by the deprivation of love and affection during psychosexual development, or that such persons may have suffered some other defect in the educational process and never fully matured morally. Some people have a low IQ and some people, in my view, have a retarded moral quotient (MQ). It is difficult to say precisely whether the causes are genetic or environmental. Fortunately, the number of totally amoral individuals is fairly small. Unfortunately, some societies themselves may be morally underdeveloped; they may encourage or condone cruelty, and they may be insensitive to violations of human rights. Under such social conditions it is far more difficult to develop an appreciation for the common moral decencies. Nevertheless, given a normal genetic endowment, I submit that most human beings have the potentiality to mature morally. Whether they do depends on their growing up in a civilized society. If they have had the advantage of developing in an enriched moral environment, where they can experience love and learn to reciprocate it and where the bonds of attachment and empathy are encouraged, they have a better opportunity to flourish morally. If the proclivity for some altruistic behavior is innate, then under optimal social conditions this has a good chance of being actualized. Young children at some point learn to go beyond their demands for infantile gratification; they learn to feel sympathy for others, to comfort them in distress, and to lend a helping hand; and they genuinely wish to share goods with their parents, sisters, brothers, and friends and to care about others besides themselves. They learn about the need for mutual support, the principles of reciprocity and fairness, and the importance of developing a sense of individual responsibility. Much of this depends upon moral training, particularly the development of good personality traits and character formation. Children thus can learn to be honest and truthful, to keep their promises, and to be kind and sympathetic, that is, to respect the common moral decencies. Some parents and teachers are prone to use authoritarian methods of reward and punishment to indoctrinate children so that they will obey the moral rules. They threaten them with sanctions or God's wrath, but it is doubtful that these methods of moral instruction are sufficient by themselves to develop an internalized sense of moral responsibility. Under optimal conditions the virtues can be instilled in young children, where they may become an integral part of the personality, nourished and strengthened by emotions.

Granted, we cannot give young children unlimited freedom to do what they want, and we need to restrain them by cultivating the virtue of rationality and self-discipline. Yet moral education that is humanistic tends to instruct by example and by positive reinforcement concerning the moral virtues, and it wishes to encourage the growth of ethical reflection. It presupposes that the moral decencies can be inculcated when positive conditions in the social environment exist for children, whose moral strivings can take root in ethically nutritious soil. Under these conditions they will more likely grow up as compassionate and altruistic beings. Although capable of individual initiative and courageous enough to fulfill their creative aspirations, they are also capable of relating to others in a caring manner and to express altruistic behavior. Thus, we need to develop in children, adolescents, and young adults a respect for the principles of ethics that transcends merely selfish or uncaring attitudes. And this can be realized in part only because of the emergence of the capacity for critical ethical thought.

COGNITION AND CARING

The roots of caring behavior are biosociogenic; they develop often unconsciously, perhaps even instinctively, and surely they are emotionally charged. At some point in human conduct, however, moral awareness is enhanced by cognition. Ethical rationality is not a superfluous addition to moral caring but can become constitutive of its very form. Because our beliefs interpenetrate and mold our attitudes, empathy and compassion may be reinforced by cognitive reflection. Indeed, it is through the process of deliberative reasoning that an individual's self-interest can be reconciled with the needs of others; intellectual factors enable us to evaluate conflicting demands within situations. In some cases, compassionate actions may be undeserving or foolish; in others, fully justifiable. In some instances, intended deeds of benevolence may be unwarranted in the light of the circumstance; in others, they may be rationally justified.

Is there a rule of reason that will help us resolve complex ethical dilemmas? Yes. There is a key ethical principle that provides us with some guidance. This takes the form of the following general rule of moral caring: *A rational person ought to express some moral caring for the needs of others.*

The first part of the principle of moral caring involves compassion and empathy. Thus, we may state as a general prescriptive rule: *Where it is within our power, we ought to mitigate the suffering, distress, pain, and sorrow of other sentient beings.* This applies to our friends and relatives, for they are within the range of our conduct. The rule also has a wider net. But there may be little that we can do for those outside our range of conduct, except perhaps to contribute to charities or agencies that will reduce hunger, assist handicapped people, and provide aid to the victims of natural disasters.

The second aspect of the principle of moral caring is that *we ought to develop a benevolent attitude toward all persons deserving of it.* Not everyone is deserving of our benevolence; those who behave indecently may be undeserving. Again, we should act benevolently where we can to those who are within our range of day-to-day conduct. And we should try to distribute goods and services in a positive way to enhance the well-being of others. For example, we ought to help children wherever possible to attend school, to learn how to think critically, to enjoy good music and the arts, and to appreciate the diverse enrichments of culture. And we ought to help ensure a prosperous and peaceful society. Thus, we also have a generalized positive moral obligation toward *all* persons. A person may accomplish this by performing little deeds or large ones, by giving gifts to individuals or charities. And he or she may also engage in cooperative social programs for the wider good.

Why do we do so? Perhaps because it is in our self-interest to do so, but also because we wish to see the good of others enhanced and to distribute to as many people who deserve it the fruits of civilized life.

In summary, this rule of ethical rationality states that *we ought to act so as to mitigate human suffering and sorrow and to increase the sum of human good and happiness, providing it is possible to do so.*

This rule is still highly controversial for many conservative libertarians. They hold that it is a mistake to dole out help to others, who instead should be taught to fend for themselves. Many libertarians oppose the role of the state in providing public welfare to the disadvantaged, the ill, needy, or elderly members of the population. They are especially opposed to the use of taxation by the state to support programs of welfare. Many would not necessarily object to other social institutions, private charities, or individuals providing assistance. Other conservatives, however, are opposed to any sustained effort at altruistic compassion and benevolence because they believe that it may undermine the virtue of self-reliance and thus foster dependency. Egalitarians, Christians, socialists, and others seek to help the weak, the poor, the homeless, and the dispossessed by distributing the goods and services of society more equitably.

Others argue that we should not simply try to divide up the existing pie but bake more and more pies. We should seek to expand economic growth rates, by providing incentives for individual achievement and entrepreneurship. All of this may be granted to some extent—though in the complex corporate world, individual enterprises have been replaced by larger economic units in which individual merit is often lost.

One might still argue on moral grounds that one ought to help those who through no fault of their own cannot help themselves. This would exclude indolent individuals who could work and prefer not to, or those who have been brought up in a culture of dependence and neither develop any independence and autonomy nor seek to pull themselves up by their own initiative.

Still another problem concerning the appropriate extent of moral caring is the fact that many conservatives today have become extremely chauvinistic or nationalistic and wish to limit the range of moral concern. They believe that their first duty is at home, not abroad. Thus, a key issue concerns the question, How far should our moral concern be extended? Should it apply to every person or community in every corner of the globe?

HUMANITY AS A WHOLE

I submit that our moral duty indeed should be extended to humanity as a whole and that this moral rule should thus be generalized. This means that we should be concerned, not only with the well-being of those within our community or nation-state but also with the entire world community well beyond our own parochial interests.

Extreme chauvinistic partiality is divisive. Although our loyalty to the norms of our country or ethnic group takes us beyond selfish parochial interests to a wider concern for the good of the inhabitants of the region in which we live, extreme chauvinism between ethnic groups and nation-states can be destructive. Moral caring thus should not end at ethnic enclaves or national frontiers. Ethical rationality enjoins us to build institutions of cooperation and to attempt wherever possible to negotiate our differences peacefully. The broader injunction is that an *impartial ethical rationality should apply to all human beings who have equal dignity and value*. This implies that we should be concerned with the defense of human rights everywhere.

Accordingly, we each have a duty to help mitigate the suffering of people anywhere in the world and to contribute to the common good, thus finding some common ground with all hu-

mans. This expresses our highest sense of compassion and benevolence. This implies that people living in the affluent nations
have an obligation to mitigate suffering and enhance the well-
being, where they can, of people in impoverished regions of the
world, and that those in the underdeveloped areas likewise have
an obligation to replace resentment against the affluent with reciprocal good will.

Chapter 5

What Do We Owe to Posterity?

CONFRONTING DEATH

We began our inquiry by raising the question, What is the human prospect? I responded that it is difficult to answer that question in abstract form. The question becomes meaningful only if it is framed in specific contextual terms, relevant to a concrete individual or a society at one time in history.

Human beings are future-oriented. We seek to peer beyond the horizons into the unknown. We are always poised, as it were, at a turning point or overlooking a brink. The religious consciousness is especially fixated on the fear of death; it creates a salvational scenario to rescue humans from nonbeing. Illnesses or accidents may strike anyone at any time. Death is the common leveler of us all, exhausting unfulfilled dreams and sorrows. "Pale death, with impartial step," said Horace, "knocks at the poor man's cottage and the palaces of kings."[1]

Unlike those who lived under previous civilizations, we have a deep awareness of the historical record. We have uncovered the

---

1. Horace, *Carminum* (*Ode*), I : 4, in *Opera* Ed. by Edvardus C. Wickham (Oxford: Oxford University Press, 1901).

remains of past civilizations; their monuments lie in ruin, and their noble heroes have long since departed. If this is the fate of all civilizations, what does the future augur for us? Can we live bereft of the illusion that we are at the center of the universe or that our civilization will withstand the inexorable erosions of history? Can we develop a realistic acceptance of our eventual decline and demise? This dilemma perhaps will help us to resolve the gnawing question of the meaning of life and the fact that none of us has an ultimate destiny.

For the average person, the consciousness of death does not have an overwhelming presence. For most, especially the young, it recedes into the background. We are focused on what will happen next. What will we do tomorrow or next week or next year? It is perhaps only when a person confronts his or her own death, or that of a loved one, that this grief may become unbearable and existential awareness exacerbated. This applies especially to poignant cases of children or young adults who are struck down prematurely or to those who die with great suffering from a debilitating disease or incapacitating accident. We can find no rhyme or reason for such tragic deaths; many of them seem unfair.

I do not see why the fact that we all will die someday need overburden us with anxiety or terror. The chief imperative, I submit, is to live well *here and now*. If one is reasonably happy, life can be enjoyable, even buoyant. Every day one can discover rich sources of excitement, no matter what one does—whether reading interesting books, going to horse races, climbing mountains, meeting beautiful women or handsome men, feasting at a banquet, working for political candidates, toiling in the gardens, coining new words, playing with the computer, reading poetry, or basking in the sun.

No doubt some individuals are so overcome with *angst* that they cannot accept death; they may lay awake nights bemoaning their fate and focus on it morbidly. Some persons may even suffer depression as a result. The key question concerns the psychology of motivation and whether the well-springs of desire can still

110

stimulate us. The psychologist John Schumaker thinks that facing the stark reality of one's own demise and that of one's loved ones is for most people too difficult to endure. Thus, the denial of death may be a necessary antidote if we are to affirm life. Schumaker maintains that sanity requires us to "corrupt reality," or else we could not function.[2] I suppose that whether one can live fully depends on the resourcefulness and staying power of the individual, and also on how the culture copes with death. That is why the *courage to become*, to live with satisfaction but also lustily and robustly, supersedes cognition and caring. For the humanist, it is not faith in eschatological myths that we require to sustain us but some realistic commitment to truth and a willingness to live with audacity and verve. I have no problem with living life exuberantly in spite of an awareness that someday I will die, nor do most of my secular humanistic friends, who have rejected belief in God yet live meaningful and exciting lives.

Is the atheist unduly harsh in the demand that everyone abandon false illusions and face the real world for what it is? Does humankind need sugar-coated pills, the proverbial opiate, to persist? Perhaps many, even most, humans need to corrupt reality to get through life, but *surely* this does not apply to all human beings, some of whom can live autonomously with an existential awareness of the human condition, its finitude and fragility as well as its opportunities and promise. Perhaps the passion for a transcendental life is so deeply ingrained in human culture or has such deep biological roots that men and women will continue to devote time and energy to venerating false Gods and sanctifying false hopes of an afterlife.

The legendary Pyramids are awesome reminders of how the Egyptians sought to deny death. Cheops, founder of the IVth Dynasty, built the Pyramid at Gizeh on the Nile, now on the outskirts of Cairo. Nearby were the tombs of his revered mother and his daughter. The Egyptian religion postulated that after death the monarch would take a journey to the underworld. Especially

---

2. John Schumaker, *The Corruption of Reality* (Amherst, N.Y.: Prometheus Books, 1994).

THE COURAGE TO BECOME

fascinating is the seagoing vessel uncovered by archaeologists after being buried for tens of centuries. This vessel was equipped with a sufficient number of sails and rowing oars to make a long journey possible. The *Book of the Dead* gave a graphic account of how to be prepared for the next life: by the mummification of the body, the offerings of food, drink, articles of the toilet, the taking of weapons, and the accompaniment of guards and servants on the voyage. That Egyptian civilization would expend such enormous energies to construct the Pyramids demonstrates how powerful the belief in immortality has been.

Christianity, with its myth of the resurrection of Jesus and its promise of salvation, likewise expresses the longing for another world. That it has survived for two millennia is added evidence of the strength of the quest for eternity and the power of the Christian narrative to slake it, however fictitious it is. This is similar for Judaism, Islam, and other religions. Even today, the least shred of "evidence" is accepted as "proof" of immortality. Reports of apparitions, of encounters with the dead, and of near-death experiences, are seized upon as testimony that there is another reality. The criticisms of skeptical inquirers that such reports are only anecdotal and have not been corroborated by the evidence all too often fall on deaf ears.[3]

It is sometimes asked, If we were to succeed in demolishing any hope for another world, would this undermine all human motivation? Not necessarily, because in many modern-day secular cultures, eschatological myths have receded into the background, at least for significant sectors of society, and new humanistic ideals have emerged to replace them. Some of these have perhaps functioned as the moral equivalent of the immortality myth for example, the belief in progress or of future utopian societies. Ever since the Enlightenment humanists have expressed optimism about the human prospect. Many believed that theistic religion in time would eventually disappear. This is based upon

---

3 . See for example Susan Blackmore, *Dying to Live* (Amherst, N.Y.: Prometheus Books, 1993) for a scientific critique of near-death experiences.

confidence in the ability of reason, science, and education to provide alternative ideals of the future.

Some critics deny this. They point to the fact that Marxism provided a secular myth as a substitute for the eschatological one and that when rigid communistic societies collapsed, the old-time religion, long thought to have been buried, only emerged in more virulent forms. They also point out that the United States, perhaps the most advanced scientific and technological society, is still burdened by theistic and paranormal myths. What this overlooks, however, is that in Western European societies, significant portions of their populations today no longer sing in the Hallelujah Chorus, instead accepting alternative secular and humanistic values.

Thus, the question can be raised: Can we frame realistic secular ideals for tomorrow that can inspire human beings throughout the world, without the need for transcendental myths? In one sense, whether we can be sufficiently motivated by secular visions of the future and whether they have the power to motivate commitment no doubt depends upon our conception of nature and of the opportunities it affords us to achieve our ends. If men and women need ideals of the future and if these are the be-all and end-all of all heroic actions and deeds, the questions are raised, *Which* ones shall we work for? *To which* ones shall we devote our lives and fortunes? Can we do *without* transcendental poetry?

FACING THE FUTURE

This brings our discussion to a critical juncture. How shall we face the future? The question of the future is relevant to our lives at every moment. Perhaps I should have changed the word to fu*tures*, for they are pluralistic. I raise here a question of basic ethical significance, for morality involves choices, that is, evaluating alternative courses of action that we wish to bring into being. This implies that we can control future events to some extent.

In one sense, human life is definitely *future-bound*. Granted, there is the present moment of awareness, the immediacy of experience that we focus on—though as soon as I concentrate on the present and seek to talk about it, it slips away. A person can recall the past, which was the present at one time. Memories of a person's past experiences provide one with some continuity and a basis for identity. I am the same person who undergoes the experiences—feelings and desires, thoughts and reflections, fulfillment and consternation. In the elusive present, I am either enjoying, enduring, or suffering some state now, or remembering things past; and I am forever looking ahead in anticipation, concerned with what will happen next. What will I do tonight? Although I live in the present and have one foot in the past, at any one moment I am always prepared to move into the future. This provides a coherent unity of who I am and what I expect in life. I am involved in preparing future events. I strive to foresee what will be; I plan to make it happen. I project constantly; my wish is father to the fact. And the same thing is true of any society wishing to know or create its future.

There is a great desire to know the future; thus, a vast industry of prophets, seers, astrologers, and psychics have flourished throughout history. Delphi illustrates the perennial importance of prophecy. Delphi was the ancient home of a legendary oracle who, it was alleged, could foretell the future. Delphi was a crossroads of Hellenic civilization, a common meeting place for the warring cities of the Mediterranean to come together in peace. The power and fame of Delphi resulted from its oracle. She responded to such queries as, "Will there be victory or defeat?" or "Will we succeed or fail in our ventures?" Her responses usually were ambiguously framed so that they could not be easily falsified. Those who asked the questions were satisfied by these enigmatic responses, or at least puzzled by their meaning. Even Socrates was alleged to have visited Diotima the seer at Delphi, who told him that "there was no one wiser in Athens."

Thus, humans constantly seek to fathom the future. Today we have our political pundits, stock market professionals, economic forecasters, diagnosticians, and meteorologists—who are often proven wrong. Nonetheless people who claim to know what will occur in the future are eagerly sought. People constantly worry about what tomorrow will bring. Many people are fearful; they dread what will ensue. "No news is good news," they say. Others are forever optimistic about future prospects. There is excitement in discovering new things, encountering daring challenges, and responding to them enthusiastically.

The questions are often raised: How future-oriented should our plans be? Should they be long-range or short-range? And there are profound moral issues: What do we owe to posterity, to future generations yet unborn, and to humanity as a whole?

FOUR IDEAS OF NATURE

The response to such questions in one sense, depends upon our cosmic outlook and whether our views of the universe are exhilarated by hope or corroded by fear. There are various ideas of nature that are relevant to our prospects for the future.

The first is the Greek concept of nature as it culminated in Aristotle's metaphysics. The central question for the Greek philosophers concerned the nature of reality. Democritus and the materialists made matter the primary reality. Plato postulated a dualism in the universe between forms, which were unchanging, and material objects in space and time, which he called appearances. The higher reality, he thought, was the realm of eternal forms. Aristotle attempted to combine both matter and form in individual substances. He allowed for both change in material substrata on the one hand, and essential forms on the other. There were regularities in nature and things happened for the most part, but there was also some room for chance. His picture of the universe was organismic; he postulated a natural teleology. The universe did not contain a theistic creator, for the universe was eternal. Although he postulated "unmoved movers," as physical principles sustaining the cosmos, such principles had no care for us. Nor did Aristotle leave room for separable, immortal souls or an afterlife, as did latter-day theists. His system left a role for practical wisdom and art, and for human intention intervening in natural processes. The universe, in any case, was intelligible to

115

reason. Human beings could understand its structure and also make rational choices.

A second idea of the universe is the Judeo-Christian-Muslim monotheistic conception of the universe. God is beyond all human understanding. He created the universe and intervenes in it miraculously. The primary obligation of human creatures is to believe in God and to obey His commandments, for which they would be rewarded or punished. Human beings are unable to solve their own problems without God. This historical drama presupposes that one accepts the doctrine of revelation expressed in the New Testament, the Koran, and other so-called sacred books. Modern philosophical and scientific critiques have undermined their credibility: salvation narratives are fictional tales contrived by human imagination to soothe the ache of death.

A third idea of nature is the Newtonian model of a material, mechanistic, and deterministic universe. Here the classical problem of free will emerges; if nature is deterministic, freedom of choice poses a problem. If everything operates by strict causal law and if there is a uniformity of the laws of nature, then there would be little room for free choice. Who we are or what we do is a product of all of the physical and chemical causes at work. If we knew them, we could make perfect predictions of every event in the future. As the future unravels, causality determines what will be. For the human species, the causes are physical, chemical, environmental, and genetic. Many philosophers have argued for a weaker reinterpretation of determinism, claiming that free choice is possible and ethically meaningful, even though it is caused. Our choices have consequences for which we are responsible. As for the mechanistic universe, God may have created the scheme of things but leaves it alone to tick away on its own, without any divine intervention. Many deists accepted the picture of God the watchmaker, though they rejected the idea of salvation or redemption.

There is still a fourth idea of nature that is prominent today, the historical evolutionary cosmos. Relativity physics and quantum mechanics have undermined Newtonian determinism. Darwin's theory of evolution has had a profound impact on our conception of how nature operates. The universe is now conceived as an open system in which chance is present. Although nature exhibits causal regularities, there are ongoing processes of change; new galaxies, solar systems, and planetary forms of life emerge. The evolutionary model thus allows both determinism and indeterminacy to play a role in the evolution of species. It also allows for the intervention by human beings in the evolutionary process. By understanding how natural processes work, we can modify conditions and act accordingly. This form of determinism does not deny the existence of causality; it simply affirms that if we know how nature operates, we can guide our own behavior in the light of it.

An earlier interpretation of the evolutionary theory exuded a form of naïve optimism. Darwinians of the nineteenth and early twentieth centuries thought that the human species was the "highest" form of life that had evolved. All lines of evolution were thought to culminate in Man. Many viewed nature as progressive. Karl Marx, who rejected a contingent universe of chance, thought that there were laws of historical determinism governing economic and social change and that if we became conscious of them, we could accelerate the dialectical process and create a utopian society. These views expressed a form of secular salvationism that has largely been discredited.

The twentieth century has undermined faith in human progress. Given two World Wars, the Nazi Holocaust, and the Stalinist Gulag, many have lost confidence in the ability of humans to solve their problems. With the growth of technology and the population explosion has come the fear that the economic system will not be able to sustain the current rapid pace of social and technological change. Apocalyptic prophecies of Armageddon abound. This pessimism is no doubt overdrawn. There is no viable alternative to the use of reason, science, and technology to solve human problems. We simply need a more realistic appraisal of their potentialities and limits.

This idea of nature as it finds expression in contemporary thought has the following implications: It allows for both causality and contingency in the universe. There is no room for a divine plan or scheme of salvation; nor is there any progressive direction to evolution. For the evolutionary model, the human species is but one among many on the planet. Nature is indifferent to what happens; we have no guarantee that our species will survive indefinitely. Nor do we have any basis for the vain hope that the individual soul will survive the death of the body.

The ongoing human prospect is that life is always ripe with challenges and full of risks; those who do not capitalize on their opportunities, or are overcome by timidity and fear, will perish. What stands out is the precarious character of human existence. The promises and dangers inherent in freedom of choice are manifold. We are responsible in part for our future; and we carry the burden of making choices and acting upon them. We can intervene in the processes of nature and control our destiny. By keeping alive, by means of medical technology, those who would otherwise die (because of our compassionate regard for them), by engaging in biogenetic engineering, and by means of environmental control, we can redirect the course of evolution. By unwise social and political policies we can destroy the habitat for future generations, or, conversely, by wise policies we can further enhance the human condition.

WHAT RESPONSIBILITIES DO WE HAVE TO FUTURE GENERATIONS?

Given this diagnosis of the human condition, we may ask: If God is dead, and if there is no guarantee of progress, why sacrifice anything for the future? Why should we care about what happens after our death when we are no longer around to witness it?

The skeptical nihilist denies that we have any obligations to future generations, maintaining that if death is truly *final*, we have no basic moral commitment. Nor do we have any rationale for life itself.

118

This view is unduly pessimistic. Countless individuals who have not believed in salvation or progress, nonetheless have evinced a strong moral concern, and also a healthy lust for life. For some persons there may be a psychological-motivational problem. There is no ultimate answer to the question *"why* live?"; life needs no justification beyond itself. The issue is not *whether*, but *how* to live, and how to live *well*. This includes the fulfillment of our goals, even after our death, so that our ideas and moral values survive our demise. This implies that our obligations extend to our children and their children, to our friends and relatives, and to the institutions that we have supported and wish to see prosper.

What is our obligation to a future world now unseen and to generations still unborn? What do we owe to them? I submit that the same moral obligation to care for humanity as a whole in the present also applies to the future of humankind. There is, as it were, an intergenerational responsibility, a continuity across generations, that a rational person recognizes. Another general rule of reason thus presents itself: *We ought to care for the future of the human species, including future generations still unborn and the planetary environment which they will inherit.* This means that *we have an extended obligation to the community of all human beings, past, present, and future.* This rule of reason grows out of and is related to the principles of moral caring, including compassion and benevolence. We can imaginatively identify with future generations and all things being equal, we ought to wish them well; surely we do not seek to harm them purposely.

This needs to be qualified in various senses. One can argue that our primary obligation is to the present (and only the immediate future), and this means that we will attempt to realize and enhance the personal, societal, and cultural values that we now cherish.

Do we have an obligation to the past? Surely in one sense we should not betray those who came before, and we should seek to fulfill our implicit promises to them. We can look back retrospectively and thank our parents and grandparents for the sacrifices

119

they made to feed, clothe, and educate our family. If we live in America, we can thank Thomas Jefferson and James Madison for the U.S. Constitution and the degrees of freedom and prosperity that they made possible for us (though it is unlikely that they could have imagined how that document would be used in future centuries). This is similarly found in other cultures or traditions.

Our primary obligation, however, is to the present world in which we live. How do we balance our obligations to the present (implied in this is the near future) with those of the long-range future? It is very difficult to do so. Often, it is virtually impossible to predict what the consequences of our actions will be on the future world. There is surely a practical difficulty with predicting or anticipating all of the effects of our actions on the indefinite future. Nevertheless, we may be inhibited from *any* action if we could take into account *all* of their long-range results on future generations. If we build a shopping mall for our convenience and use, will we have destroyed a forest in the process, which will be needed in the future? If we squander fossil fuels now, will we in time exhaust this resource entirely? Should we use it only sparingly today? If so, should future generations be allowed to use it, or are *they* likewise also obligated to preserve it for future generations *ad infinitum*? How far into the future shall we base our decisions? If very far, perhaps we will conclude that no one should use any resource. Conversely, should we care only about our needs today and allow future generations to come up with their own solutions to the problems we have bequeathed them? Who can say what kinds of sociopolitical systems will exist in the future and what kinds of virtues they may cherish? Perhaps they will not be free democratic societies; perhaps their values will be alien to ours.

Although as rationally prudent persons we focus primarily on present needs and interests and those of the immediate future, we nonetheless should have some concern for future generations. We should not be impervious to the effects that our actions may have on the environment and on future generations.

It may be asked, How can we be said to have an obligation to nameless and faceless persons in the future? How can they be said to have rights against us, if they do not as yet exist? My response is that a right is a claim made by a person on another person or institution. If that person is as yet unborn, then the right exists as a *potential* right in recognition of the likelihood that such a claim in the future may be made. Thus, we can make a case that those still to be born have implicit rights and claims against us.

We can look back and retrospectively evaluate the actions of our forebears, and we can praise or blame them for their acts of omission or commission. We can criticize, for example, those who cut down the rain forests in Brazil. We can thank the architects and engineers for the fine water treatment plants, underground disposal systems, highways, and bridges that they built and are used today with profit. Thus, we can empathize with a future world and imaginatively project what those who will live then may be like, and we can infer obligations today for those tomorrow. Our obligations to the future stem in part from our gratitude and appreciation (or perhaps condemnation) of generations previous to ours and the sacrifices they made, for which we benefit. Thus, future persons need spokespersons today serving as their proxies and defending their future implicit, potential rights. It can therefore be argued that we do indeed have some obligations to the future.

At the very least a general ethical principle emerges: *Do nothing that would endanger the very survival of future generations of the human species and of their habitat.* And another principle follows from this: *We should use what we need rationally and avoid wasting nonrenewable resources.* To so argue is not to impose an impossible obligation because a good portion of the human race already is morally concerned about future posterity, including an environmental concern. We should thank our forebears who sacrificed themselves in battles against oppression or who created revolutions to preserve liberty and justice. One might argue that it was for their own generation, but I would say it was also for posterity. Countless men and women have struggled to ensure a more

121

peaceful, healthful, and democratic world; they have attempted to build better institutions so that their fellow human beings could prosper. One may even argue that the heroic idealism devoted toward a beloved cause beyond themselves and for the greater good of humanity has always inspired human beings. Thus, a viable humanistic ideal focusing on a better world can engender ethical commitment, without need for any theistic foundations.

CURRENT PROSPECTS

At the present juncture of history, a number of streams of global change are rapidly converging. These point to ominous dangers but also to unparalleled opportunities.

Population is expanding; in some portions of the globe it is virtually unchecked. Can the planet continue to support this unlimited growth? Is it not prudent to try to restrain population growth by means of birth control? Some religious dogmatists are opposed to contraception, but this opposition could be countered by adopting wise measures of population control. Increasing population is an enormous drain on natural resources, which are being depleted at a heady pace. It is made possible by improved technologies, which have increased food production and lowered the death rate. Natural environments, however, including rain forests and water resources, are being exploited and polluted. Many species, unfortunately, are becoming extinct because of overexploitation. Technology has vast potentiality to change the condition of human nature by genetic engineering, and of the natural ecology by altering the environment. There are unforeseen dangers in these developments as well as unparalleled opportunities. For example, technology has led to the proliferation of powerful weapons of mass destruction (nuclear, biochemical, and so on) which someday may be unleashed and may destroy human and other forms of life on the planet. Yet at the same time there are enormous positive opportunities that emerging future technologies can tap.

Free-market economies are productive, but they are often impervious to the common good. Future generations have a right to clean air and water, the integrity and continued existence of the natural landscape, a fair share of the planet's depleted resources, and safety from genetically-transmitted diseases. They should have spokespersons as proxies today who can restrain the destruction of large areas of the globe. Some environmentalists are so worried about possible abuses of the natural ecology that they maintain scientific and technological development needs to be severely curtailed. Martin Heidegger believed that a major problem that we face is the uncontrolled growth of technology. Many postmodernists are pessimistic about our ability to fulfill the ideals of the Enlightenment. They have lost faith in science and reason and believe that there are no epistemological standards of objectivity. They reject humanism, freedom, autonomy, and they have little confidence in the ability of humans to solve problems and to contribute to a better world. This is a new form of nihilism.

Is it time to call a halt to scientific, technological innovation and change? Should we seek to restrain scientific research and development? Would that help reduce population and restrict further environmental degradation? Should, or indeed could, humankind return to an earlier idyllic past?

Unfortunately, it would be difficult to do so in any massive way. We cannot simply repeal the present world. Our option is not to stamp out technology or to radically restrict it, as modern-day Luddites might desire, but to develop it wisely and to introduce new technologies that will include safeguards against further noxious effects. It is clear that the human species is often endangered, that the environment has limited carrying capacity, and that at some point we will need to restrict population and restrain uncontrolled technological proliferation. But it would be folly to call for a complete halt—for there are still vast uncharted and auspicious horizons. It is the courageous ingenuity of humankind that can create new vistas still unimagined and can build a better tomorrow for everyone that should be encouraged. Indeed, it is the tremendous opportunities for human good that technology can offer which we need to keep in sight. The entire history of human civilization may be functionally interpreted in the light of technological breakthroughs. This began with the discovery of fire, the invention of the flint stone, the wheel, the domestication of animals, agriculture, the construction of roadways and cities, the digging of mines and wells, and the creation of seagoing vessels. During the Industrial Revolution great breakthroughs were achieved, including the invention of steam power, the locomotive, and machine manufacturing. In the twentieth century we have witnessed the invention of the automobile, air travel, radio, and TV. And in the postindustrial age we have seen such marvels as the computer, robotics, antibiotics, artificial limbs, biogenetic engineering, and space travel.

The technologies still waiting to be discovered are unknown, yet they hold forth great promises for Prometheans unbound who have the courage and intelligence to develop them and the moral caring to use them wisely for human good.

HUMAN TRANSCENDENCE: THE GREAT ADVENTURE

The challenge is hurled again: *Why* should we want a better tomorrow? Why should we care about what will occur in 2150 or 5150? What if humans were again reduced to a cave-like existence? Why is the creation of cultures better than the primitive existence of food-gatherers or hunters? It is perhaps presumptuous from our standpoint to declare that earlier modes of human existence were inferior. After all, the human species and its precursors persisted for millions of years before the emergence of civilizations. One can go even further and ask, Why should a person care if the human species, in any form, survives?

I submit that it is incumbent on rational persons to be concerned about the continuity of the stream of human life in the future. Can I prove that ethical principle? Can one *prove* any ethical principle? Perhaps not. If we cannot prove it, however, we can at least make a *reasonable* case for it. The universe for us now and, imaginably, for future generations would be a better place if the human species were to survive than if not. A universe with future Michelangelos and Beethovens, Marie Curies and Jane Austens, Confuciuses and Buddhas, Picassos, and Galileos would be far preferable than one without them. Value is relative to human needs, interests, and desires; from the human standpoint, then, the human species ought to survive and flourish because there is a deep yearning that we do so. A mature and healthy moral consciousness recognizes this imperative.

Is this a transcendental goal? To talk about future generations yet unborn surely transcends a person's present moment of experience, and it takes us beyond the present sociocultural context to an indefinite future. Yet it is not transcendental in any supernatural sense, for it does not take us out of the natural world. True, the future is unpredictable and unknown at any one time, and it is only an imagined future state. Who could have imagined among the first settlers who came to the Americas in the seventeenth century that in three centuries the pioneers would have forged their way to the west coasts of North and South America? Who could have known in the year 1900 that humans would someday fly to the moon and back; that they would conquer diseases, such as polio and tuberculosis; that both India and China could have developed the wherewithal to prevent famine and feed their vast populations; and that with the information revolution, every corner of the world community would be able to communicate instantaneously with every other part? We cannot easily predict what will occur in human civilizations of the future, what fate will befall them, or what great adventures will unfold.

Nevertheless, an ethical concern that there *be* future human civilizations is of *transcendent* importance to us as humans today. It is of no importance to an indifferent universe at large, nor to a nonexistent Deity. As humanists, we reaffirm that the be-all and end-all of human life is *the survival and the flourishing of life itself*. It is justified in the heroic struggling, battling, enjoying, and living it. The fact that human beings cherish their own survival and those of their fellow human beings instinctively and cognitively is reason enough for this cardinal ethical principle; and it is the reason why we can extend moral caring, compassion, and benevolence not only to the present human condition but also to future states of humankind.

The great human adventure is to live creatively and exuberantly. Human life provides its own rationale; it needs no justification beyond itself. That is the humanistic message, and it is the challenge of the human prospect in every age. The most exciting way to cope with life requires that we cherish the courage to become, the capacity to reason, and the ability to care for other human beings. In every age, there are new and unchartered seas to voyage across, new forms of culture to create. Having conquered the planet, our next mission perhaps is to conquer our solar system and to explore the unknown dimensions of the universe beyond. There is no final end to human history, no stopping point, no final resting place. There is only a future, which we will have some role in forging and creating. Each age requires the fortitude to survive, to persist, to fulfill its plans and projects, and to prosper. No one can predict with certainty what lies ahead. That is the essence of the human adventure: to face challenges boldly, to think critically and to have some altruistic ethical regard for the entire human family.

Courage is still the first humanistic virtue; it is out of this fearless posture and because of it that men and women were able to leave the caves of primitive existence and to build civilizations. It is the continuing human adventure that captivates and enthralls us. It is the very essence of what it means to be human, the creative impulse venturing forth into the world and stamping the mark of humanity upon it. If the human species is to survive and embark upon exciting new voyages and adventures, it will be only because it still can marshal the determination to take responsibility for its own destiny and the courage to fulfill its unique ideals and values, whatever they may be. It will always need *the courage to become.*

Selected Bibliography

SELECTED BOOKS PUBLISHED BY PAUL KURTZ

Decision and the Condition of Man. Seattle: University of Washington Press, 1965. Paperback edition, New York: Dell Publishing, 1968.

Humanist Manifesto II. Amherst, N.Y.: Prometheus Books, 1973.

The Fullness of Life. New York: Horizon Press, 1974.

Exuberance: A Philosophy of Happiness. Los Angeles: Wilshire Book Company, 1978.

A Secular Humanist Declaration. Amherst, N.Y.: Prometheus Books, 1980.

The Transcendental Temptation: A Critique of Religion and the Paranormal. Amherst, N.Y.: Prometheus Books, 1986.

Forbidden Fruit: The Ethics of Humanism. Amherst, N.Y.: Prometheus Books, 1988.

Eupraxophy: Living without Religion. Amherst, N.Y.: Prometheus Books, 1989.

Philosophical Essays in Pragmatic Naturalism. Amherst, N.Y.: Prometheus Books, 1990.

The New Skepticism: Inquiry and Reliable Knowledge. Amherst, N.Y.: Prometheus Books, 1992.

Toward a New Enlightenment: The Philosophy of Paul Kurtz. Edited by Vern L. Bullough and Timothy J. Madigan. New Brunswick, N.J.: Transaction Publishers, 1993.

SELECTED BOOKS EDITED BY PAUL KURTZ

American Thought before 1900: A Sourcebook from Puritanism to Darwinism. New York: Macmillan, 1966.

American Philosophy in the Twentieth Century: A Sourcebook from Pragmatism to Philosophical Analysis. New York: Macmillan, 1966.

Sidney Hook and the Contemporary World: Essays on the Pragmatic Intelligence. New York: John Day, 1968.

Moral Problems in Contemporary Society: Essays in Humanistic Ethics. Englewood Cliffs, N.J.: Prentice-Hall, 1969.

Tolerance and Revolution: A Marxist-non-Marxist Humanist Dialogue. With Svetozar Stojanović. Belgrade: Philosophical Society of Serbia, 1970.

Language and Human Nature: A French-American Philosopher's Dialogue. St. Louis, Missouri: W. H. Green, 1971.

A Catholic-Humanist Dialogue: Humanists and Roman Catholics in a Common World. With Albert Dondeyne. London: Pemberton Books, 1972.

The Humanist Alternative: Some Definitions of Humanism. London: Pemberton Books; Amherst, N.Y.: Prometheus Books, 1973.

Sidney Hook: Philosopher of Democracy and Humanism. Amherst, N.Y.: Prometheus Books, 1983.

A Skeptic's Handbook of Parapsychology. Amherst, N.Y.: Prometheus Books, 1985.

Building a World Community: Humanism in the Twenty-First Century. With Rob Tielman and Levi Fragell. Amherst, N.Y.: Prometheus Books, 1989.

OTHER WORKS CITED

Aristotle. *Poetica*. In *The Works of Aristotle*. Ed. and tr. by W.D. Ross. Oxford: Oxford University Press, 1950–1952.

Bacon, Francis. *Novum organum*. In E.A. Burtt, ed., *English Philosophers from Bacon to Mill*. New York: Modern Library, 1939.

Bayle, Pierre. *Pensées diverses sur la comète: édition critique avec une introduction et des notes*. Ed. by A. Prat. Paris: Hachette, 1911–1912.

Beloff, John. "What Is Your Counter-Explanation? A Plea to Skeptics to Think Again." In Paul Kurtz, ed., *A Skeptic's Handbook of Parapsychology*. Amherst, N.Y.: Prometheus Books, 1985.

——. "The Skeptical Position: Is It Tenable?" With replies by James Alcock, Susan Blackmore, Martin Gardner, Ray Hyman, and Paul Kurtz. *Skeptical Inquirer* 19, no. 3 (May/June 1995).

Bierce, Ambrose. *The Devil's Dictionary*. New York: Hill and Wang, 1961.

Blackmore, Susan. *Dying to Live*. Amherst, N.Y.: Prometheus Books, 1993.

Blake, William. *The Marriage of Heaven and Hell*. London: Trianon Press, 1960.

Brontë, Emily Jane. "No Coward Soul Is Mine." In Janet Gezari, ed., *Emily Jane Brontë: The Complete Poems*. London: Penguin Books, 1992.

Burton, Robert. *Anatomy of Melancholy: What It Is, with All the Kinds, Causes, Symptoms, Prognostics, and Several Cures of It*. Boston: William Veazie, 1859.

Cowper, William. *The Task*. Philadelphia: Tower & Hogan, 1826.

Dante Alighieri. *The Divine Comedy*. Boston: D.C. Heath & Co., 1909.

Dewey, John. *Theory of Valuation*. Chicago: University of Chicago Press, 1939.

Dickinson, Emily. *The Complete Poems*. Boston: Little, Brown and Company, 1924.

Dryden, John. *Mac Flecknoe*. Oxford: Clarendon Press, 1924.

Emerson, Ralph Waldo. "Self-Reliance." In *Emerson's Complete Works*. Boston: Houghton, Mifflin and Company, [nd.].

Feyerabend, Paul. *Against Method*. New York: Schocken Books, 1977.

Flew, Antony. *The Politics of Procrustes*. Amherst, N.Y.: Prometheus Books, 1981.

Gay, John. *Fables*. Menston: The Scolar Press, 1969.

Gibbon, Edward. *The Autobiography*. New York: Dutton, 1911.

Hook, Sidney. "Naturalism and First Principles." In *The Quest for Being and Other Studies in Naturalism and Humanism*. New York: St. Martin's Press, 1961.

Horace, *Opera*. Ed. by Edvardus C. Wickham. Oxford: Oxford University Press, 1901.

James, William. *Memories and Studies*. New York: Longmans, Green, 1911.

——. *The Will to Believe*. New York: Longmans, Green, 1927.

Landrum, Gene. *Profiles of Genius*. Amherst, N.Y.: Prometheus, 1993.

——. *Profiles of Female Genius*. Amherst, N.Y.: Prometheus, 1994.

Lorenz, Konrad. *On Aggression*. New York: Harcourt, Brace and World, 1966.

Mead, George Herbert. *Mind, Self, and Society from the Standpoint of a Social Behaviorist*. Edited by Charles W. Morris. Chicago: University of Chicago Press, 1956.

Nagel, Ernest. "Naturalism Reconsidered." In Paul Kurtz, ed., *American Philosophy in the Twentieth Century*. New York: Macmillan, 1966.

Neuhaus, Richard John. "The Public Square: A Continuing Survey of Religion and Public Life." *First Things: A Monthly Journal of Religion and Public Life*, no. 42 (April 1994).

Nietzsche, Friedrich. *Thus Spake Zarathustra*. Tr. by Thomas Common, rev. by H. James Birx. Amherst, N.Y.: Prometheus Books, 1993.

Pope, Alexander. *Essay on Man*. London: L. Gilliver, 1734.

Popper, Karl. *The Open Society and Its Enemies*, vol. 1: *The Spell of Plato*. London: Routledge & Kegan Paul, 1945, revised 1952;

vol. 2: *The High Tide of Prophecy: Hegel, Marx, and the Aftermath*. London: Routledge & Kegan Paul, 1945, revised 1952.

Rorty, Richard. "Pragmatism without Method." In Paul Kurtz, ed., *Sidney Hook: Philosopher of Democracy and Humanism*. Amherst, N.Y.: Prometheus Books, 1983.

Russell, Bertrand. *Unpopular Essays*. New York: Simon and Schuster, 1950.

Schumaker, John. *The Corruption of Reality*. Amherst, N.Y.: Prometheus Books, 1994.

Shakespeare, William. *Julius Caesar*. In *The Works of Shakespeare*. New York: The Macmillan Company, 1903.

———. *Macbeth*. In *The Works of Shakespeare*. New York: The Macmillan Company, 1905.

Tagore, Rabindranath. *The Crescent Moon*. London: Macmillan, 1913.

Thackeray, William Makepeace. *Vanity Fair: A Novel without a Hero*. Oxford: Oxford University Press, 1983.

Thomas, Dylan. "Do Not Go Gentle into That Good Night." In *Selected Poems*. Ed. by Walford Davies. London: Everyman, 1993.

Tillich, Paul. *The Courage to Be*. New Haven, Conn.: Yale University Press, 1952.

Voltaire, François-Marie Arouet. *A Philosophical Dictionary*. New York: Coventry House, 1932.

Wilson, E.O. *On Human Nature*. Cambridge, Mass.: Harvard University Press, 1978.

Index

Index

Burton, Robert, 98

Caligula, 102
Caring, 3, 37, 81–85, 87, 88–91,
    93–95, 97, 101, 103, 104, 106,
    119, 124
Carneades, 14
Carthage, 77
Catherine the Great, 29
Chauvinism, 106
Cheops, pharaoh, 111
Christian Coalition, 68
Christianity, 31, 42, 73, 84, 85,
    97, 112
Churchill, Winston, 17
Cognition, 3, 40, 43, 49, 53, 58,
    60, 61–63, 67, 73, 75, 77, 80,
    85, 104, 111
Cognitive science, 60
Combots, 62
Common moral decencies, 1,
    80, 101–103
Common sense, 57
Communication, 80
Communism, 31, 41, 113
Compassion, 78, 82–86, 89–92,
    94, 95, 97, 103–105, 107, 118,
    119
Conservatism, 76
Copernican revolution, 6
Courage, 3, 10, 19, 22, 23, 25, 26,
    30, 32, 33, 35–37, 42, 72, 73,
    75, 79, 81, 97, 103, 111, 123,
    124, 126
Creationism, 53
Creativity, 29, 32, 58, 97
Critical thinking, 57–60, 63, 80,
    103
Cruelty, 98, 99, 101, 102

Cultural relativity, 17
Culture, 20, 80
Curie, Marie, 17
Curiosity, 56
Custom, 49
Cynicism, 17

Dahmer, Jeffrey, 102
Dante Alighieri, 27
Darwin, Charles, 17, 117
Darwinian revolution, 6
Darwinism, 53
De Gaulle, Charles, 17
Death, fear of, 109, 110
Democracy, 39
Democritus, 115
Descartes, René, 14
Desire, 21, 61
Despair, 13, 17
Determinism, 116, 117
Dewey, John, 39
Dickinson, Emily, 82
Diotima, 114
Dissent, 41
Dostoevsky, Fyodor
    Mikhailovich, 17
Dryden, John, 16

Edison, Thomas Alva, 29
Egocentric predicament, 61
Egoism, 88, 95–97
Egypt, 44
Einstein, Albert, 17, 29, 32
Eliot, George, 32
Emerson, Ralph Waldo, 31
Empathy, 78, 81, 82, 86, 87, 90,
    91, 94, 95, 102, 104
Empiricism, 40, 42
Enlightenment, 11, 14, 112

Index

Index

Index

Pyrrho, 14

Quantum mechanics, 116

Rationalism, 40
Rationality, 56, 57, 70, 73, 74, 78, 79, 85, 103–106; contextual or contingent, 68, 69, 79; radical, 77; reformist, 75, 79
Reason, 37, 39, 40, 42, 47, 49, 51–53, 56, 60, 67, 70–73, 76
Reliable knowledge, 14
Responsibility, 81, 102, 118, 119, 126
Revelation, 12, 40, 52, 53, 116
Roman Catholicism, 44
Rome, 16
Roosevelt, Franklin Delano, 17
Rorty, Richard, 55, 56, 57
Rourke, Bill, 34, 35
Russell, Bertrand, 41, 49

Sakharov, Andreí, 31
Salvation, 14, 17, 24, 31, 37, 95, 96, 109, 112, 116–119
Santayana, George, 44
Sartre, Jean-Paul, 20
Schopenhauer, Arthur, 31, 35
Schumaker, John, 111
Scientific method, 53, 56, 57
Scientism, 56, 57
Secularism, 25
Self-reliance, 88, 105
Seneca, Lucius Annaeus, 35
Sexist attitude, 32
Sextus Empiricus, 14
Shakespeare, William, 8, 35
Shelley, Percy Bysshe, 17

Skepticism, 14, 49, 50; constructive, 14, 50; extreme, 47; total negative, 14
Socialism, 31
Socrates, 31, 39, 70, 71, 114
Solzhenitsyn, Aleksandr, 31
Sophocles, 17
Speer, Albert, 64
Spiritualism, 45, 46, 54
Spirituality, 13, 53; medieval, 11
Stalin, Iosif Vissarionovich Dzhugashvili, 78, 102
Stoicism, 72
Subjectivism, 17, 63, 70
Suicide, 35

Tagore, Rabindranath, 88
Tautology, 48
Technology, 21, 53, 55, 57, 117, 122, 123, 124
Teleology, 9
Territorial imperative, 99, 100
Tertullian, Quintus Septimius Florens Tertullianus, 42
Thackeray, William Makepeace, 90
Theism, 11, 14, 24, 25, 27, 37, 40, 42, 54, 59, 63, 72, 95, 112, 116
Theology, 52, 59, 85
Thomas, Dylan, 20
Thrasymachus, 71
Tillich, Paul, 23
Totalitarianism, 67
Tradition, 49
Transactional theory, 61
Transcendental temptation, 17
Troy, 16
Trustworthiness, 2

Index

Turner, Ted, 29
Twain, Mark, 17

Utilitarianism, 95

Verdi, Giuseppe, 91

Voltaire, François-Marie
  Arouet, 17, 43
Will to believe, 40
Wilson, E. O., 86
Wright, Richard, 32

About the Author

PAUL KURTZ is Professor Emeritus of Philosophy at the State University of New York at Buffalo. He is editor of *Free Inquiry* magazine, Chairman of the Committee for the Scientific Investigation of Claims of the Paranormal, and former Co-President of the International Humanist and Ethical Union. He has authored and edited over thirty books, including *The Transcendental Temptation; Forbidden Fruit: The Ethics of Humanism*; and *The New Skepticism*.